THE ASSERTIVENESS HANDBOOK

MARY HARTLEY is a writer and personal development coach specializing in people skills and communication. She has considerable experience of writing on these topics and of presenting workshops and courses on aspects of interpersonal communication and behaviour. As well as contributing to national newspapers and women's and general-interest magazines, Mary has broadcast on national and local radio programmes on issues such as managing anger and coping with stress, and has acted as consultant for the BBC Learning Zone. Her books *The Good Stress Guide, Managing Anger at Work, Body Language at Work* and *Stress at Work* are all published by Sheldon Press.

D0338994

Overcoming Common Problems Series

Selected titles

A full list of titles is available from Sheldon Press,
36 Causton Street, London SW1P 4ST and on our website at
www.sheldonpress.co.uk

The Assertiveness Handbook
Mary Hartley

Breaking Free
Carolyn Ainscough and Kay Toon

Cataract: What You Need to Know
Mark Watts

Cider Vinegar
Margaret Hills

Coping Successfully with Irritable Bowel
Rosemary Nicol

Coping Successfully with Panic Attacks
Shirley Trickett

Coping Successfully with Ulcerative Colitis
Peter Cartwright

Coping with Anxiety and Depression
Shirley Trickett

Coping with Blushing
Professor Robert Edelmann

Coping with Bowel Cancer
Tom Smith

Coping with Brain Injury
Maggie Rich

Coping with Childhood Allergies
Jill Eckersley

Coping with Chronic Fatigue
Trudie Chalder

Coping with Dyspraxia
Jill Eckersley

Coping with Gout
Christine Craggs-Hamilton

Coping with Polycystic Ovary Syndrome
Christine Craggs-Hinton

Coping with Postnatal Depression
Sandra L. Wheatley

Coping with Thyroid Problems
Dr Joan Gomez

Curing Arthritis – The Drug-Free Way
Margaret Hills

Curing Arthritis Diet Book
Margaret Hills

Depressive Illness
Dr Tim Cantopher

Eating for a Healthy Heart
Robert Povey, Jacqui Morrell and Rachel Povey

Free Your Life from Fear
Jenny Hare

Help Your Child Get Fit Not Fat
Jan Hurst and Sue Hubberstey

How to Accept Yourself
Dr Windy Dryden

How to Cope with Difficult People
Alan Houel and Christian Godefroy

How to Keep Cholesterol in Check
Dr Robert Povey

The Irritable Bowel Diet Book
Rosemary Nicol

Letting Go of Anxiety and Depression
Dr Windy Dryden

Living with Alzheimer's
Tom Smith

Living with Asperger Syndrome
Dr Joan Gomez

Living with Autism
Fiona Marshall

Living with Fibromyalgia
Christine Craggs-Hinton

Living with Food Intolerance
Alex Gazzola

Living with Rheumatoid Arthritis
Philippa Pigache

Living with Sjörgren's Syndrome
Sue Dyson

Losing a Baby
Sarah Ewing

Losing a Child
Linda Hurcombe

Overcoming Jealousy
Dr Windy Dryden

Understanding Obsessions and Compulsions
Dr Frank Tallis

Overcoming Common Problems

The Assertiveness Handbook

Mary Hartley

sheldon PRESS

First published in Great Britain in 2005

Sheldon Press
36 Causton Street
London SW1P 4ST

Copyright © Mary Hartley 2005

British Library Cataloguing-in-Publication Data

A catalogue record for this book is available from the British Library

ISBN 0–85969–941–2

1 3 5 7 9 10 8 6 4 2

Typeset by Deltatype Limited, Birkenhead, Merseyside
Printed in Great Britain by
Ashford Colour Press

Contents

1

What is Assertive Behaviour?

You've been cornered and asked to take on something that you really don't want to do. It could be something like helping at a charity fund-raising event. You open your mouth to say no, and a few minutes later find that not only have you agreed to run a stand, but you've offered to organize a raffle and a tombola as well. Or you want to raise a difficult issue with someone at home or at work, but you back away from bringing it up because you don't want a row, or you are scared of how the other person may react, or you don't trust yourself to speak without getting angry, tongue-tied or bursting into tears. Or perhaps you have experienced occasions when you have dealt with a difficult situation by dropping hints about what you are thinking or feeling, then felt annoyed and frustrated because your hints were ignored. Does all this sound familiar?

They are all examples of non-assertive behaviour. Instead of expressing your thoughts and needs in a direct and appropriate way, you say things you don't mean, or you don't say the things that are on your mind, perhaps because you are scared of the consequences, perhaps because you can't find the right words. However, you can change the way that you think and behave. Assertiveness is a set of skills that can be learnt. You can learn to behave assertively, and to develop skills that will enable you to communicate confidently and appropriately in all situations and so enhance your effectiveness in your personal and professional life.

Sometimes aggressive and over-pushy behaviour is described as assertive. This is a misconception. Behaving in a punchy way to get what you want is at the other end of the scale from giving the impression that you are willing to let the world walk all over you. Assertion focuses on communicating and managing situations in a confident way that shows respect for yourself and for other people. It means expressing yourself clearly and showing that you want to work with others to find the best solution. Behaving assertively doesn't mean that you will always get your own way, but it will generally lead to better results, more understanding and mutual respect.

Think about those people who you trust and respect. It is likely that they are open and straightforward in their dealings, that they are calm and reasonable in discussion and that they can express positive and negative feelings clearly and honestly. In short, they behave assertively.

Learning to behave assertively will bring you great benefits. You will have greater self-respect and will in turn be respected by others. You will feel confident in your ability to handle conflict, to say no, to ask for what you want, to give and receive praise without feeling awkward and embarrassed, and to say difficult things without hurting yourself or the other person. Just think – no more silent fuming because you think you can't say how you're feeling about something, no more kicking yourself for not having said no to a request, no more being about to hand in your notice because you feel you can't broach a difficult topic with your manager. Becoming assertive takes effort and practice, but it is well worth the trouble.

Assertiveness is a type of behaviour based on self-respect and respect for others. It means handling situations and people with confidence and self-assurance, while respecting others' feelings and acknowledging their rights. Assertive behaviour demonstrates that as people we are all equal, and that we can express our needs, opinions and feelings openly and honestly.

An important idea to grasp is that assertiveness is not about winning, but about communicating and finding solutions that encompass the needs and rights of everyone concerned. It means that you are in control of yourself and situations, but not that you wish to control other people. Behaving assertively means not slighting or hurting others, and not allowing them to slight or to hurt you.

The core of assertive behaviour is a philosophy which honours the worth of human beings and their right to be treated with respect.

Rights and responsibilities

Assertiveness is based on an understanding and acceptance of certain rights which we all share. These rights are to do with self-acceptance and self-respect, and acceptance of and respect for others. You could add your own examples to this list.

I have the right to be treated with respect.
I have the right to change my mind.

I have the right to make mistakes.
I have the right to say no.
I have the right to ask for what I want.
I have the right to be listened to.
I have the right to my own feelings.
I have the right to my own beliefs.
I have the right to express my feelings and beliefs.
I have the right to be wrong.
I have the right to admit ignorance.
I have the right to express anger.
I have the right to choose not to be assertive.
I have the right not to take responsibility for other people's feelings.

Your own examples:

1 _____

2 _____

3 _____

Some myths about assertiveness

Myth: In general, assertive people are not liked.
Reality: The opposite is true. Most of us like dealing with people who are honest and straightforward without being hurtful, who are fair and who treat us with respect.

Myth: Only certain kinds of people can be assertive. I'm just not like that.
Reality: Assertiveness refers to behaviour, not to personality. Our behaviour is learnt. We aren't born with the knowledge of how to behave, we learn it through a variety of processes. The good thing about this is that our behaviour can be changed and we can learn new ways.

Myth: It isn't polite to be assertive.
Reality: This perception is based on the idea of politeness as superficial manners, and sees assertiveness as impolite behaviour

because it is based on honesty and directness. It is true that assertive communication is not based on maintaining peace and pleasantness at all costs, but in fact behaving assertively towards other people shows them respect and treats them as equals. Rudeness and abruptness are not characteristics of assertiveness. One of the skills of assertive communication is being firm and forthright when necessary without being rude or impolite.

Myth: Assertive people want to get their own way all the time.
Reality: Assertion is not about getting your own way – that type of behaviour is aggressive, not assertive. Assertive behaviour is about communicating needs clearly and openly without pushing for personal gratification at the expense of the other person.

Myth: Assertive people are bossy.
Reality: Assertive people are prepared to use authority when it is appropriate. They are secure enough to delegate authority to others.

Myth: Assertive women are unfeminine.
Reality: This is an outdated stereotypical view of women and of femininity, which also shows a lack of understanding of what assertiveness is.

Myth: Assertive people get what they want.
Reality: Behaving assertively does not mean that you will get your own way, but it makes it more likely that you will get a good outcome for yourself and the others involved.

Exercise: Assess your assertiveness

Mark how confident you feel about dealing with these situations and behaviours. 1 is low and 9 is high.

Stating your view clearly	1 2 3 4 5 6 7 8 9
Disagreeing with someone senior to you	1 2 3 4 5 6 7 8 9
Disagreeing with your partner or spouse	1 2 3 4 5 6 7 8 9
Giving criticism	1 2 3 4 5 6 7 8 9
Responding to criticism	1 2 3 4 5 6 7 8 9
Dealing with former peers who you now manage	1 2 3 4 5 6 7 8 9

Saying no without feeling guilty	1 2 3 4 5 6 7 8 9
Giving praise	1 2 3 4 5 6 7 8 9
Receiving praise	1 2 3 4 5 6 7 8 9
Dealing with aggressive behaviour	1 2 3 4 5 6 7 8 9
Dealing with passive behaviour	1 2 3 4 5 6 7 8 9
Dealing with manipulative behaviour	1 2 3 4 5 6 7 8 9
Handling conflict	1 2 3 4 5 6 7 8 9
Dealing with people who disagree with you	1 2 3 4 5 6 7 8 9
Responding to a put-down	1 2 3 4 5 6 7 8 9
Dealing with tension/conflict	1 2 3 4 5 6 7 8 9
Expressing displeasure	1 2 3 4 5 6 7 8 9
Delegating work	1 2 3 4 5 6 7 8 9
Using effective body language	1 2 3 4 5 6 7 8 9
Add your own examples:	
_____	1 2 3 4 5 6 7 8 9
_____	1 2 3 4 5 6 7 8 9

Barriers to assertive behaviour

The reasons for our behaviour are often very complex. They may stem from our childhood, from the way we were treated by parents and other adults, from the messages we were given. Think about the mental barriers that could be making it difficult for you to behave assertively.

Barrier: Negative thoughts

Many of the factors that prevent us from behaving assertively are rooted in our thoughts and feelings about ourselves and other people. These thoughts are often based on assumptions and not experience, and they can reflect our lack of confidence in ourselves and our ability to handle relationships and communicate effectively. We send ourselves negative messages about the way our behaviour will be received and we allow these irrational thoughts to trap us into unhelpful ways of thinking.

Some common types of negative thinking are:

- *Making assumptions about other people and situations.* When we jump to conclusions about what is going on in other people's minds and how they will react, we think ourselves into a situation which makes assertive communication very difficult. This is what we do when, for example, we assume that someone who passes by without saying hello is ignoring us. We might take it even further and assume that the person is ignoring us because of something we have done or said.

- *Deciding the future.* Sometimes we behave like fortune-tellers who can foresee the future. 'There's no point in asking,' we think, 'because he will only say no.' We think, 'If I don't drop everything I'm doing to listen to my friend's problems whenever she wants then she will think I'm awful and hate me.' This pattern of thinking prevents us from behaving assertively and encourages us to be passive in situations where an active approach would be more productive.

- *Filtering out the positive.* Hearing only the negative part of things which are said to us is a common type of distorted thinking. For example, if you are told that you gave a good presentation but it could have been shorter, you think, 'I made a real mess of that – it was far too long.' Another way of discounting the positive is diminishing a compliment or praise or positive feedback with a statement like 'Anyone could have done that', or questioning the sincerity of what is said.

Sort out your thoughts

You can overcome the barriers presented by various kinds of negative thinking in the first place by recognizing in your own behaviour any of these unhelpful patterns. Use these questions to help you identify how valid your thoughts are:

- Is this thought based on facts and evidence?
- Is this thought taken to an extreme, rather than being a moderate response?
- Does this thought help or hinder a confident, assertive approach?

Once you have recognized the nature of your response, you can change your way of thinking by replacing it with a more helpful statement.

Scene: Lucy thinks she will sound stupid

Lucy has recently joined the local drama group and is at a

meeting to discuss the programme for the coming year. She has some ideas she would like to suggest, but there are a few very forceful personalities putting forward their views, and when the Chair of the meeting asks for other contributions, Lucy shrinks back into her seat. She tells herself that her ideas would just sound silly.

Lucy convinces herself that she cannot contribute to the meeting because other people will think that what she has to say is silly or stupid. Lucy has no way of knowing if this is true or not, but she allows the thought to prevent her from speaking out.

Lucy can overcome this barrier by learning to question and challenge her negative thoughts and replace them with more positive ones.

Negative thought: They will think my ideas are stupid.
Positive thought: Why would they think that? Have these people ever indicated that they think of me that way? I know that my proposals aren't silly.

Negative thought: I might get one of my facts wrong and look ignorant.
Positive thought: Will it matter that much if I make a mistake or have some inaccurate information? It's all right to be wrong sometimes. We are all human.

Exercise: Challenge your negative thoughts

Think of three situations where this kind of negative thinking prevents you from acting assertively. For each example, replace your negative thought process with a more helpful self-talk.

Situation	Negative thought	Positive thought
e.g. Making the first move to greet an acquaintance.	I'll seem pushy.	Why should I be seen as pushy? I'm being friendly.

1 _____

2 _____

_____

3 _____

_____

Taking things personally

When we take things personally we interpret other people's behaviour as being focused on ourselves, and believe that their actions and feelings are caused by us. This kind of thinking prevents us from communicating assertively because we quickly persuade ourselves that there is no point in speaking up because the other person has already made up his or her mind.

Scene: Tom thinks it's all about him

Tom has an argument with a friend at work, and later sees that friend deep in conversation with someone else. Tom thinks, 'He's obviously talking about our row and turning everyone against me.' Later on he sees his boss frowning as they pass each other, and he thinks, 'She must be annoyed with me because I asked for a day off.'

Tom could change his way of thinking. Instead of: 'She is annoyed because of me', he could say to himself, 'She may be annoyed because of my request, she may be annoyed because of something else. I will not make an assumption that affects the way I communicate with her.'

Barrier: Fear of consequences

Sometimes we are prevented from behaving assertively because we are scared of the reaction our behaviour might elicit. Lucy at her drama group is nervous of what might happen if she speaks up. She does not think rationally about what it is that she fears, she just lets these vague apprehensions influence her behaviour.

Lucy can learn to talk through her fear of consequences. She can ask herself questions such as, 'What might happen if I speak up?' This could lead on to the reply, 'Some of the people there might

WHAT IS ASSERTIVE BEHAVIOUR?

rubbish my ideas.' Once she faces this possibility, Lucy can take it further and think, 'What if some people do? It is only their opinion.'

Exercise: Getting consequences into perspective

Try making yourself say out loud what consequences you fear if you behave assertively in particular situations. (Sometimes, just saying the words can make you realize how irrational the fear is.) Ask yourself how likely the consequence is. Then ask yourself questions such as, 'So what? Just how much would that matter? What would happen as a result of that?'

Situation	Fear of consequences	Challenging questions/ statements
e.g. Asking for help.	The person will resent me.	Is that likely? I'm making a legitimate request. If the person does resent what I say, we can talk about the situation.
1		
2		
3		
4		
5		

Barrier: Imagining the worst possible scenario

Sometimes we create a barrier to behaving assertively by taking our fear of consequences to the furthest point. However, this tendency can actually help to overcome the barrier, because the process of working through the consequences to the most extreme conclusion can put the situation in perspective.

Lucy could imagine the very worst that could happen as a result of her contributing her ideas. Everyone could ridicule them. They might all laugh at her for coming up with such stupid suggestions. They could say that she is not clever enough to be a member of the association and demand her immediate resignation. By taking the possibilities to a ridiculous extent Lucy can see that nothing awful will happen if she speaks up, and even if the very worst were to occur, so what? She could live without being in this particular drama group, especially if its members are so unreceptive of new ideas. This process of thinking makes Lucy see that her fears are irrational, and gives her the confidence to behave more assertively.

Barrier: Inflexible ideas

You might have some beliefs about your own and others' behaviour that have developed over the course of your life and are so ingrained that you are hardly aware of them. Some of these beliefs may be based on notions of what is and isn't acceptable behaviour, and they are reflected in thoughts such as 'It's not right to . . . ' or 'I should always . . . '

If your thinking is full of shoulds, musts and oughts you may be unable to acknowledge your true feelings because you are trapped by a set of limiting beliefs that hinder your ability to behave assertively.

Scene: Craig is annoyed with Jason

Every week Craig and Jason meet for a drink, and Jason is always late. He has a different excuse every time, one which seems genuine, and is very apologetic.

'Sorry, mate,' he says this evening. 'The phone went just as I was leaving. You know how it is.'

'That's okay,' says Craig. He feels annoyed, but thinks that he should not express his feelings. He bottles up his annoyance, and behaves quite grumpily. When Jason asks him what is wrong, Craig shrugs and says, 'Nothing.'

Craig could change his attitude and give himself permission to express his feelings. Accepting that it is all right to feel annoyed and to say so is vital to assertive communication.

Craig and Jason will have a better relationship if Craig can say what's on his mind and hear Jason's response. As it is, they both feel uncomfortable.

Exercise: Getting rid of unhelpful ideas

Identify any of your unhelpful 'shoulds' and 'oughts' that may limit your ability to behave assertively. Replace them with statements that will encourage you to assert yourself.

Unhelpful thought   *Helpful thought*

e.g. You should keep quiet when   It's fine to say when you are
you are annoyed.   annoyed.

1 _____

2 _____

3 _____

4 _____

5 _____

6 _____

Barrier: The way you interpret situations and behaviour

The way you see a situation and construct its meaning is coloured by many factors: your ideas about the world, your beliefs and assumptions, your personality, your feelings and expectations. No two people will see the same situation identically. Everything we perceive is subject to a process of selecting, organizing and interpreting the information that our senses absorb. We see what we want to see or expect to see, we see what interests us and filter out what to us is irrelevant information. Then we make the information fit our view of life and our own unique, individual position. There is nothing wrong with this process – it is the only way we can make sense of the barrage of information we have to deal with. If, however, you assume that your interpretation is the only correct one, you limit your ability to empathize with others and you can be constrained by faulty beliefs about other people's behaviour.

11

Benefits of behaving assertively

Assertive behaviour will enhance and improve every aspect of your life. You will benefit from:

- *Taking responsibility for yourself.*
  This is a highly significant benefit, and one that will transform the way you feel about yourself and the way you relate to other people. Accepting responsibility for your own thoughts, feelings and actions gives you great personal strength and instantly improves the way you communicate with others. You do not blame or rely on other people for your emotional state, but you own your feelings and are prepared to make changes in order to get a better outcome.

- *Stating what you want openly and honestly.*
  Once you get used to communicating like this you will wonder why you ever put up with biting your tongue, feeling scared to speak or dropping hints that may or may not be picked up.

- *Being prepared to compromise.*
  One of the characteristics of assertive behaviour is being able to resolve difficulties and disputes in a way that is comfortable and fair to yourself and others. When you accept that compromise and negotiation are viable and desirable components of dealing with other people, your levels of tension and anxiety drop and you will find that you can communicate calmly and effectively, without pushing inappropriately for your own needs or caving in.

- *Listening to others.*
  Active listening is a skill of assertive communication that leads to improved relationships, deeper understanding, better problem-solving and meaningful communication.

- *Increased self-confidence.*
  You will deal with other people and challenging situations much more effectively, and you will become aware of feeling more confident in your ability to respond appropriately in any circumstances. You will notice that you are taken more seriously by others, and you will see a change in the way that they deal with you.

- *Greater self-awareness.*
  The whole process of identifying and expressing your feelings leads to greater self-knowledge, which helps you to communicate clearly and honestly.

12

- *Feeling better for having expressed your feelings.*
  Expressing thoughts and feelings appropriately is a great stress-reliever. Bottling things up is not healthy, and can lead to an explosion of irritation or anger if you get to the point where you feel you can't keep quiet any longer. It is much better to get problems off your chest in a controlled and assertive way.
- *Giving and receiving criticism confidently and effectively.*
  The skills of handling criticism assertively will help you to build productive relationships based on openness and fairness.
- *Giving and receiving praise effectively.*
  The quality of your relationships in every aspect of your life will be improved by the exchange of positive feedback. You can learn how to acknowledge and affirm other people openly and straightforwardly, and how to accept others' affirmations of you.

Exercise: What will you gain?

What are the particular advantages for you of behaving more assertively? Complete the following statement with as many examples as you like.

Behaving more assertively will mean that:

1 _____

2 _____

3 _____

4 _____

5 _____

6 _____

Making a choice

Finally, just because you *can* be assertive doesn't mean that you *have* to be. Remember that assertion is a way of behaving. We can learn how to behave in this way and we can make the choice to adopt an assertive style of behaviour and communication. This does not mean that assertion is always the best option, or that we are obliged to act assertively. Having a certain right does not mean that you need to exercise it all the time. You have the right to choose. Once you are confident in yourself, and are familiar and comfortable with a range of behaviours, then really it is up to you to choose how you want to react in particular circumstances.

You have the choice to adapt your behaviour to suit the situation. If you want to access another style of behaviour, go ahead. You might think that there are times when throwing a quick temper tantrum or a fit of the sulks pays off, or there may be certain circumstances in which you might decide it is just not worth disagreeing or expressing your point of view or fighting your corner. Or you could be apologizing for something and it might suit the circumstances and the personalities involved for you to deliberately exaggerate how sorry you are and what you will do to make up. This is not being self-abasingly passive, it is expressing your feelings in a light-hearted, humorous way which you judge to be appropriate for the situation. Similarly, if you don't understand what someone is trying to explain, you could deliberately adopt a 'I'm really thick and slow, so please give me the directions one more time' approach.

Always check, though, that your decision is based on sound thinking and that you are not backing away from an assertive response out of misplaced fear, lack of confidence or because of any of the other barriers we looked at earlier. The important thing is not to let self-doubt or anxiety prevent you from behaving in the way that you want.

You will find the ability to communicate assertively enormously beneficial in your dealings with friends, colleagues, family and others.

Making the right choice

Exercise: Should I take an assertive approach?

It is a good idea to assess difficult situations in terms of how much they really matter to you. Try using this chart to judge how you should respond. Any situation that gets a high ranking and is unlikely to change probably requires you to take assertive action.

WHAT IS ASSERTIVE BEHAVIOUR?

Situation	How much it bothers me	How likely is it to change?
1 ——————————	1 2 3 4 5 6 7 8 9	1 2 3 4 5 6 7 8 9
2 ——————————	1 2 3 4 5 6 7 8 9	1 2 3 4 5 6 7 8 9
3 ——————————	1 2 3 4 5 6 7 8 9	1 2 3 4 5 6 7 8 9
4 ——————————	1 2 3 4 5 6 7 8 9	1 2 3 4 5 6 7 8 9
5 ——————————	1 2 3 4 5 6 7 8 9	1 2 3 4 5 6 7 8 9
6 ——————————	1 2 3 4 5 6 7 8 9	1 2 3 4 5 6 7 8 9

Behaving more assertively will affect your personal and professional relationships. A change in your behaviour will bring about a change in the way you are perceived and the way others react to you. These changes will be for the better, bringing many benefits. You should be prepared for a possible initial negative reaction from those who have benefited from your lack of assertion in the past, but with your enhanced communicative skills you should be able to deal with this situation effectively should it arise.

Assertive behaviour will not only help you to handle everyday and challenging situations, but will also lead to healthy and positive relationships in every aspect of your life. As you practise the skills of assertive behaviour you will grow more confident in your ability to deal with situations openly and appropriately in a way that brings self-respect and respect from others.

2

Styles of Behaviour

Often we do not acknowledge that we have choices about how we behave in situations. We have become used to certain patterns of behaviour and response that are now characteristic of us.

Exercise: How do you behave?

This quiz will help you find out what type of behaviour you usually exhibit. Decide which of the following descriptions is most like the way you normally behave. Tick the appropriate response for each question and then work out your score.

1 You are out for a meal with a work or social group you belong to. You are hard up at the moment, so have only a starter and some mineral water. When the bill comes, the group splits it evenly between everyone there. Do you:
   (a) Pay the amount that is requested – it would be embarrassing to say anything.
   (b) Say something like 'This is really unfair. I hardly ate or drank anything. I don't see why I should subsidize everyone else'.
   (c) Say something like 'I'm happy to pay (state fair amount) for my contribution.'
   (d) Pretend you've just realized that your credit card has expired, so that someone will have to pay for you.

2 A friend asks you to swap the school run on a day when you are free to do it, but you don't want to. Do you:
   (a) Say you can't because you have to go out, and hide in the kitchen in case she sees that you are in all day.
   (b) Agree to do it, because you'd feel really awkward if you didn't, and kick yourself for not having refused?
   (c) Say something like 'I do my fair share already, you know, and I do have a life.'
   (d) Say something like 'I have to say no on this occasion, but I'll swap next week if you like.'

16

3 A position at work has suddenly become vacant, and you would very much like the job. Do you:
   (a) Wait until it is advertised.
   (b) Tell your manager that you are the obvious choice and they would be crazy not to give you the job.
   (c) Ask for a meeting with your manager to put your case.
   (d) Make jokey comments about what a good job you would do, hoping that your hints will be picked up.

4 At work, your boss asks you to speak to one of your team about her unsatisfactory work. He has to go to a meeting and can't do it himself. You think there are some factors about the person's work that should be taken into account. Do you:
   (a) Say something like 'Actually, it's not my job to talk to her.'
   (b) Say something like 'Oh well, I suppose I can, if that's what you want.'
   (c) Say something like 'I understand that you haven't got time today, but I would like us to discuss her work before either of us says anything.'
   (d) Say yes, planning to find that you will be too busy to actually do it.

5 Your teenage daughter wants to go to a very late function on a school night. You remind her of your agreement about school nights and say she can't go. She then asks your partner, who gives his/her permission to attend the function. Do you:
   (a) Say furiously that your partner has no right to undermine you in this way and you will lock your daughter in her room if necessary.
   (b) Say that they are really upsetting you and you can feel a migraine coming on.
   (c) Prepare yourself to compromise on this occasion, but say that you would like all three of you to discuss how to apply the rules you have agreed, and speak to your partner privately about how let down you felt.
   (d) Give in. Anything for a quiet life.

Scoring

1	(a) W	(b) P	(c) L	(d) T
2	(a) W	(b) T	(c) L	(d) P
3	(a) W	(b) P	(c) L	(d) T

4 (a) L	(b) W	(c) L	(d) T
5 (a) P	(b) T	(c) L	(d) W

If you scored mostly Ps, this indicates that your behaviour tends to be Punchy, or aggressive. If you scored mostly Ws, this indicates that your behaviour tends to be Wimpish, or passive. Mostly Ts suggests that you behave in a Tricky or manipulative way. The L answers refer to the kind of Level behaviour that is assertive.

Being punchy

Scene: Martin's aggressive manner

'Well, that's not going to work!' says Martin at the weekly team meeting. 'I would have thought it was obvious that this option will take too long and be too expensive. And apart from that . . . ' He jabs his finger forward as he makes several further points, and raises his voice and speaks more forcefully when other people indicate that they would like to say something. At the end of the meeting he says, 'This has been a ridiculous waste of time', and bangs the door behind him as he leaves.

We have all experienced punchy, or aggressive behaviour. It is likely that many of us have responded aggressively in certain situations. The instinct to hit out in order to attack someone or to defend ourselves is a deep-rooted response; in prehistoric times it enabled our ancestors to secure the survival of our species. When we are faced with a challenge, our system responds by preparing us to deal with it – our heartbeat rises, our breathing becomes shallow, our legs shake, our fists clench. Our body is preparing for a fight, and we are ready to lash out, physically or verbally. In some circumstances, this is a healthy and helpful reaction. In most everyday circumstances, it is neither of these things.

What lies behind aggressive behaviour

The attitude that informs aggressive behaviour is the belief that your rights are more important than anyone else's. People who behave aggressively are determined to get their own way regardless of what

18

others might think, feel or want. They come across as dominating and hostile, and seem to be always on the attack.

Sometimes this type of behaviour masks insecurity and lack of confidence. It may be that aggression is a way of covering up inner fears and anxieties. It is also possible that a person who behaves aggressively does not know any other way of responding, and has not learnt the skills of dealing appropriately with people and situations.

Typical thoughts and attitudes that are linked with aggressive behaviour

There are winners and losers in life and I'm not going to be a loser.

There's no point in being Mr or Ms Nice Guy if you want to get results.

Someone has to make the decisions round here.

Someone has to get a grip on what's going on.

I'll show them.

No one's going to push me around.

It's important not be seen as weak.

Examples of aggressive behaviour

Being determined to get your own way.

Riding roughshod over others.

Forcing people to do what you want.

Not listening.

Making arrangements that you know will be unpopular but allowing no discussion.

Pushing people into a corner about something.

Not accepting or ignoring a refusal.

Interrupting conversations because you want to be heard.

Talking over people.

Making threats, even jokingly.

Swearing.

Dismissing other people's ideas and contributions.

Ridiculing others.

Being unwilling to explain.

Being unwilling to negotiate.

19

Aggressive body language

Aggressive behaviour is often fuelled by the adrenalin rush that leads to forceful and threatening body language. Aggression is signalled by gestures such as pointing or jabbing with your finger, clenching your fists, banging the table or drumming with your fingertips. Aggressive posture is tense and strained, sometimes with arms crossed or hands on hips. Crowding someone else's personal space can be a sign of aggression, whether it is standing too close in order to intimidate, or spreading yourself and your possessions so that they take over a supposedly shared space. Frowning and glaring are often seen to be aggressive, as is staring someone down.

Aggressive ways of speaking

Shouting or speaking inappropriately loudly and stridently is often aggressive, but so is speaking very, very quietly in a way that can imply a threat, and makes people strain to hear you. Sarcasm is an aggressive tool, like any form of humour designed to mock or put someone down. Words and phrases which, depending on the context, can be aggressive include:

> If I were you . . .
> That's rubbish!
> You would say that, wouldn't you?
> I don't care what you say.
> You've changed your tune!
> I've heard it all now.
> You will do this because I say so.
> I don't know where you get your ideas from.
> Don't try that on me.
> Oh, come on!
> Isn't it obvious that . . .
> Surely you can't believe that . . .

Advantages of aggressive behaviour

Of course there are some benefits to aggressive behaviour. In the short term, it can get results, and can give an illusion of power and decisiveness. Sometimes people who are seen to behave aggressively are promoted to positions of authority, which seems to reward this style of behaviour. Aggressive people are often perceived as being able to get what they want, materially and emotionally, and in a competitive society they seem to exhibit the behaviour of a winner.

Disadvantages of aggressive behaviour

However, in the long term, aggression does not lead to healthy, positive relationships. The aggressive boss may have been promoted in spite of his or her aggressive style, not because of it. An aggressive style of management in the workplace may result in a culture in which people are scared to admit mistakes or misunderstandings, and just want to cover their own backs. An aggressive person might get his or her own way, but it will be at the expense of other people's respect, and, ultimately, it will be damaging to their own self-respect. After losing your temper or delivering an angry, aggressive outburst, you may experience guilt, shame and embarrassment. Not only this, but people in teaching, leading or nurturing roles who habitually use this style of behaviour and communication are likely to stunt and stifle the development of those in their charge, who may well feel intimidated and inhibited from expressing their own thoughts and ideas.

Being tricky

Scene: Amy pulls people's strings

Amy slams the door of the flat and throws her bag on to the floor. She makes herself a cup of coffee and drinks it in the kitchen by herself, ignoring the others in the sitting room. Eventually one of her flatmates comes into the kitchen and says, 'Why are you sitting in here by yourself? Is something wrong?'

'No', says Amy shortly. She flounces past and goes up to her room. The others feel uncomfortable and wonder what has upset her.

A short time later Amy smiles sweetly at her flatmate and says, 'Can I borrow your black top tonight? It looks so stunning on you, and I haven't got anything decent to wear for this dinner.'

Amy's behaviour is manipulative. Manipulative behaviour is a way of getting our needs met while avoiding direct communication about the issue. Occasionally we all play games in order to get what we want. Perhaps we say something to someone who we hope will pass it on to the appropriate person because we don't want to say it face to face. Or we pretend to be in agreement with a plan but then pick holes in it to others, or find ways of making sure it doesn't work. Anyone who drops hints and hopes they are picked up could be said to be behaving manipulatively. We send messages that are not clear and we expect other people to interpret our meaning. Manipulative behaviour is a kind of emotional blackmail through which we try to control others in an indirect way.

What lies behind manipulative behaviour

Behind manipulative behaviour lies the belief that your rights are more important than anyone else's, but you are not going to let them know that. This kind of tricky behaviour is a form of indirect aggression, because it is based on the desire to get one's own way and to make one's feelings known, but not directly. We may respond with this kind of behaviour when we feel strongly about something, but do not know how to express our feelings appropriately. We may feel scared of direct disagreement or confrontation.

Sometimes people behave manipulatively out of a desire to be popular and well-liked, which leads them to flatter and keep in with others. They say things they don't mean and pretend to listen to and be concerned about other people's opinions and situations, when in fact they are motivated purely by self-interest. People who behave manipulatively mislead others about the nature of their relationship. Manipulative behaviour can show a need to control others, but in a way that is not overtly aggressive and so protects one's self-esteem. It is possible that a habitual manipulator has low self-esteem and feelings of inferiority, which he or she masks with a show of confidence.

Typical thoughts and attitudes that are linked with manipulative behaviour

When I don't want to do something, I'll agree to keep in with the person, then 'forget'.
You can get people to do what you want by making them feel guilty.
I'll throw a bit of a wobbly.
I'll find a way of getting back at him/her.
I can twist him/her around my little finger.

22

I'll give them the silent treatment.

The best way to deal with people is to tell them what they want to hear.

I'll turn on the charm.

Examples of manipulative behaviour

Sulking.

Sabotaging someone's work.

Sabotaging someone's plans.

Revealing something told to you in confidence.

Gossiping.

Playing politics.

Letting people think you agree with them and saying the opposite when they are not around.

Pushing people's guilt buttons.

Exploiting knowledge of people's soft spots to get your own way or make them feel uncomfortable.

Tactical flirting.

Holding grudges.

Looking for ways to get your own back on people.

Manipulative body language

Someone in manipulative mode may use body language to mask his or her real feelings. Posture can be over-relaxed, and gestures such as touching the arm might be used to give an impression of friendliness. Other examples are showing displeasure by flouncing, slamming doors and deliberately isolating oneself from a person or group. Typical of this kind of behaviour is smiling and being pleasant to someone's face, then as you turn away raising your eyebrows or pulling a face for others to see.

Manipulative ways of speaking

People behaving manipulatively use language to create an impression rather than to communicate directly. Hinting and insinuating are common tactics, and so are insults and put-downs which are disguised as jokes. Words and phrases which, depending on the context, can be manipulative, include:

23

You're a star!

I don't know what I'd do without you.

You're the only person I could trust with this.

I'm not mentioning any names, but several people have complained.

Come on, that was a joke!

I'm only doing this because I care for you/love you/am concerned about you.

This is for your own good – I'm not getting anything out of it.

Advantages of manipulative behaviour

There are short-term advantages to this kind of behaviour. You can feel better for having given vent to your feelings, and you can always tell yourself that you are not doing anything overtly aggressive. Sometimes indirect communication works, and in some circumstances it may be appropriate to rely on hints to get your message across.

Disadvantages of manipulative behaviour

Manipulative, tricky behaviour is a form of aggression, so it is not surprising that people who behave in this way can experience the same kind of guilt and shame that often follows aggressive outbursts. If you are moody and unpredictable, people are likely to steer clear of you or keep you at arm's length in order to protect themselves, and you could become quite isolated. Playing games with others and using emotional blackmail is not likely to lead to strong, positive relationships in your personal or professional life. Expressing your emotions indirectly and using verbal and behavioural techniques to undermine people and put them down leads to a life characterized by coldness and hostility.

Being wimpish

Scene: Naomi doesn't say what she wants

Naomi has had a frustrating day. At work she couldn't join her friends at lunchtime because at the last minute her boss said, 'Could you just be around to answer the phone for half an hour? I've got to pop out for something.' She was out of the door before

Naomi could speak, not that she could say anything, of course. After work she had planned to do a big shop in the out-of-town mall, but discovered that her son had taken the car – again – without asking her. 'He won't even dream of putting any petrol in it', she thinks.

Just as she is sitting down in the evening to watch her favourite TV programme the phone rings. It's a friend who has had a row with her partner and wants to talk about it. Naomi turns the sound down and listens to her, twisting her mouth and tapping her foot in annoyance.

Naomi is behaving in a passive way. Most people behave passively sometimes. Many of us have experienced circumstances in which we find it difficult to express our thoughts or our needs; in some situations, we automatically put ourselves last and allow the needs of others to overrule our own requirements. Sometimes we respond passively to challenges and stressful situations as a way of keeping out of trouble and protecting ourselves. Passive or submissive behaviour is what we exhibit when we do not take responsibility for ourselves, and allow other people to put themselves first and to decide on our behalf what we are thinking and feeling. We behave self-effacingly, and act in the way that we think will please other people rather than assert ourselves.

What lies behind passive behaviour

Submissive behaviour sends the message that everyone else's rights are more important than yours. You may well have low self-esteem and be anxious that people should like you. You do not do or say anything that you think might bring a negative response from others, and this fear of imagined consequences limits your communication. Pleasing others is your way of gaining approval and acceptance. You avoid disagreement and conflict because you see it as aggressive behaviour.

Typical thoughts and attitudes that are linked with passive behaviour

Anything to keep the peace.
I can't say no.
They will think I'm awful if I . . .
It's not polite to . . .

25

It's not very nice to . . .

I hate scenes.

I can't do/say this because he or she will be hurt/be angry/not like me.

It's wrong to put yourself first.

I don't like unpleasantness.

It's not nice to be pushy.

It's wrong to show off.

People should not be angry with me because I never show anger to them.

It's best not to rock the boat.

Other people should be nice to me because I am nice to them.

Examples of passive behaviour

Not saying what you want.

Apologizing when you haven't done anything wrong.

Being unable to say no.

Putting yourself down.

Acting like a martyr.

Moaning and complaining.

Being reluctant to express a preference.

Not committing yourself to an opinion.

Being reluctant to make decisions.

Giving in to what other people want.

Self-pity.

Not answering the phone/avoiding people because you can't handle a situation.

Passive body language

In this kind of behaviour, the whole body seems to become submissive – it's as if the person is apologizing for taking up space on the planet. Posture is slumped and low, with hunched shoulders. Your hands cover the mouth, or are clasped tightly together. You tend to sit or stand with your legs twisted around each other, and your arms are often clasped tightly across the front of your body in a defensive gesture. Eye contact is uncertain and evasive, as if you are scared of looking directly at someone. Passivity is shown through nervous gestures such as fidgeting and twiddling with or nervously stroking your hair. You may well smile nervously when you are expressing annoyance or when you are being criticized or told off for something.

Passive ways of speaking

The speech patterns of someone behaving passively are strongly characterized by uncertainty and hesitation. You apologize a lot, and find it hard to say anything directly. Instead, you go all round the houses with explanations and justifications. You use fillers such as 'um' or 'er' when you speak, and habitually make statements such as 'You know what I mean' and 'sort of thing'. Words and phrases which, depending on the context, can be passive, include:

> I'm really sorry to bother you.
> Sorry for being such a nuisance.
> Would you mind terribly if . . .
> It's just that . . .
> I know I'm being stupid, but could you explain . . .
> Would it be all right if . . .
> I don't suppose you'll agree, but . . .
> It's only my opinion.
> I'm probably speaking out of turn.

Advantages of passive behaviour

Behaving passively is a way of keeping the peace, for a short time at least. It means that you do not become involved in conflict or arguments, you do not put other people out by refusing to do what they ask, and people will not disagree with you because you do not voice opinions that are different from theirs. Because you avoid making decisions, you will never make one that is unpopular. You may be thought of as nice, easygoing or accommodating, and your show of weakness could lead others to protect and take care of you.

Disadvantages of passive behaviour

On the other hand, you may be seen as a pushover, someone who can always be persuaded (or bullied) into agreement. You are unlikely to win people's respect, nor are you likely to respect yourself. Your difficulty with saying 'no' could lead you to take on too much and put yourself under stressful pressure. You bottle up feelings of resentment and anger at being used and taken for granted, and there is the possibility that these feelings will build up and finally be expressed in an emotional outburst or explosion of rage, or lead to stress-related illnesses. Rather than thinking how nice you are, it is possible that your friends, family and workmates might be annoyed and frustrated by the way that you don't say what you want and won't make a decision.

Being assertive

Scene: Beth's mother visits
Beth's mother tuts with disapproval as the children watch television.

'They watch far too much rubbish,' she says. 'If I were you I would make them use their time more productively.'

Beth takes a deep, calming breath and makes her face and shoulders relax. On several occasions during her mother's stay Beth has been annoyed by the constant criticisms of the way she is bringing up the children, and she thinks that this is the moment to say something.

'I know you have their best interests at heart,' she says, 'but you know, Mum, I'm not doing a bad job bringing up the children, and they're turning out pretty well. I feel undermined when you find fault with the way we do things.'

Later on Beth receives a phone call from a friend she plays badminton with asking her to take part in a tournament. 'You're such a good player,' her friend says. 'We're bound to do well with you on the team.'

Beth likes playing badminton, but thinks that while her mother is staying it would be best not to take on this kind of commitment. She does not want to leave her mother alone too much. 'Thanks for asking me,' she says, 'but I'm going to have to say no this time. If there's another tournament later in the year, I'd be very interested in making up the team.'

Her friend sounds annoyed. 'Well, we were all relying on you. We stand much less chance of winning now.'

Beth says, 'Sorry you were relying on me. As I said, do ask me again later on. Anyway, I'll see you at the club night as usual next week.'

Beth is behaving assertively. She expresses her thoughts and feelings appropriately, in the right way to the right people. She does not blame others, but takes responsibility for herself and acknowledges and owns her feelings. Beth is able to respond calmly and confidently without becoming worked up and angry, and she does not allow other people to put pressure on her. Here we see her dealing effectively in two potentially difficult situations, criticizing her mother and saying no to a friend who is annoyed and disappointed by her refusal. In both cases she is not deflected from her intention, and makes her position clear without giving offence, being rude or caving in. She could have chosen not to say anything to her mother and perhaps just let off steam to a sympathetic friend, or let the situation build up until she lost her temper with her mother, maybe damaging their relationship in a way that could be difficult to rectify. She could have allowed guilt at letting down her badminton friends to force her to agree to the request, or have apologized profusely for her decision and felt bad about saying no. Many of us find that we are able to deal assertively only with certain people and situations. However, we can learn to apply similar behaviour in any circumstance, once we have learnt the basic principles and practices.

What lies behind assertive behaviour

Assertive behaviour is founded on self-esteem and self-acceptance. If you like yourself, it matters less that others should like you, and you can communicate with people pleasantly and directly, without being hungry for approval or needing to establish your superiority. Being at ease with yourself encourages others to be at ease with you. From a secure basis of self-worth, the assertive person responds to others as equal to equal. Assertive people communicate in a way that demonstrates their sense of self and at the same time acknowledges and respects others.

Typical thoughts and attitudes that are linked with assertive behaviour

I would prefer people to act in certain ways, but I accept that they do not have to.
If I make a mistake, I can handle it and move on.
It is all right to feel angry.
No one can force me to feel or behave in a certain way.
I cannot force others to feel or behave in a certain way.

29

Honesty is important.
I do not deliberately hurt others.
I am reasonably happy with myself.
I can learn how to deal with difficult situations.
What's the worst that can happen?
I know that I can choose how to behave.
I am responsible for my own feelings.
I did that well.
That was hard for me to say. I'm pleased I did it.

Examples of assertive behaviour

Saying no without feeling guilty.
Looking for solutions rather than victory.
Confronting difficult behaviour.
Being able to bring things into the open.
Stating your own needs and preferences.
Giving praise and compliments.
Apologizing appropriately.
Listening actively.
Being able to ask for help.
Being able to separate the behaviour from the person.
Not taking everything personally.
Accepting a refusal or rejection without feeling personally slighted.
Accepting justified criticism.
Being able to give criticism.
Being able to disclose and communicate your feelings.
Showing respect for others' feelings.
Initiating conversations.
Disagreeing with others' opinions.
Not allowing others to hurt or control you.
Being assertive even when others behave non-assertively.

Assertive body language

Assertive body language is confident and relaxed. When you behave assertively your posture is upright and steady, and you keep at an appropriate distance from the other person, showing understanding of and respect for personal space. Your gestures are open and you make direct eye contact. Your tone of voice and facial expressions match the words that you are using – you frown when you are serious or angry, and smile when you are pleased. Your communication is clear and consistent.

Assertive ways of speaking

Words and phrases which, depending on the context, are assertive, include:

How do you feel about that?
My experience is . . .
Can we discuss this?
How does that sound to you?
My feelings are . . .
What about if we . . .
I would like to . . .
From my point of view . . .
The way I see it . . .
I'd like to hear your views on this.
I feel strongly about this issue.
I'm not willing to . . .
I'm not prepared to . . .
How can we sort things out?
What would you prefer?

Assertive language is accurate and positive. It uses words and phrases that establish a basis of equality and suggest an expectation that there will be a positive outcome to the encounter.

An assertive person does not ask for permission to speak to people, to ask a question, to ask for help. He or she does not use phrases such as 'Sorry to bother you' but, having gained the attention of the person, goes straight in with 'Laura, there is something I need to ask you' or 'Mick, I'd like to talk something over with you. Is this a good moment?'

Advantages of assertive behaviour

The key advantages of assertive behaviour are more self-respect, and more mutual respect and understanding in your dealings with others. You are more likely to create and foster fulfilling relationships in every area of your life because you are not influenced and hindered by feelings of anxiety and fear. This style of behaviour increases your choices and helps you to break away from damaging, limiting or stereotypical ways of dealing with people.

Challenges of assertive behaviour

People are likely to be more open and honest with you, and it may take some time to adjust to this. There is often some risk for both the parties involved in self-disclosure and in acknowledging areas of conflict.

If it has been your habit to get what you want come what may, by applying direct or indirect pressure, you will need to become accustomed to a more collaborative and inclusive approach. Changing from a submissive or aggressive way of behaving may well involve some personal struggle, as you move on from the familiar habits of communication that have worked for you in the past. You will need to learn, practise and develop new skills of listening and negotiating, and this can be very challenging.

Changing your behaviour

The descriptions we have looked at apply to the ways in which we behave, not to our personalities. It is more than likely that to some extent we have all displayed each type of behaviour at some point. It is helpful to find out what style we usually adopt when dealing with certain people and challenging situations, and if appropriate decide to change the way we react. Behaviour is a set of skills, which we acquire through the complex processes of socialization as we watch and imitate, and we can learn new skills and ways of behaving. Although people sometimes say things like 'I can't help it, I'm the kind of person who just has to speak my mind', or 'I could never go through that kind of interview', the fact is that none of us is born shy, or confident, or aggressive or passive; we can change and develop different characteristics. Even habitual, instinctive behaviour, like making a journey you do regularly or walking around your home or workplace, can be changed in a very short space of time – think how quickly you adapt to a different journey, a different home, a new place of work. Usually, in just a matter of days you no longer turn left because that's where the bathroom in the old house was, or automatically set out to travel by your former route to work. With new skills and behaviours, practice is the key to success, as anyone knows who has ever learnt something new, whether it is mastering a language, a new computer programme, a new recipe, or assembling or building something.

Just as your behaviour pattern adapts quite quickly to new situations and you can learn and practise new skills, in the same way you can learn to behave assertively, and replace unhelpful ways of behaving with positive patterns of speech and behaviour.

Exercise: Behaviour in difficult situations

When you are unhappy or unsettled about the way that you are dealing with a situation, think first of all about what kind of behaviour is being shown towards you. Then think about what kind of behaviour you are demonstrating. Find some words and phrases that describe your words and actions and those of the other person involved. Then think about the way you would like to behave.

You could focus on some of the situations you identified at the end of Chapter 1, the ones that really bother you.

Situation ⸻

What other person says ⸻

How other person behaves ⸻

Behaviour type ⸻

What I say ⸻

How I behave ⸻

Behaviour type ⸻

How I would like to behave ⸻

Situation ⸻

What other person says ⸻

How other person behaves ⸻

Behaviour type ⸻

What I say ⸻

How I behave ⸻

Behaviour type ⸻

How I would like to behave ⸻

Situation ⸻

What other person says ⸻

How other person behaves ⸻

Behaviour type ⸻

What I say ⸻

How I behave ⸻

Behaviour type ⸻

How I would like to behave ⸻

Once you have identified how each of you is behaving, you can decide how you want to deal with it. You can choose and practise a different way of behaving and responding. The worst choice in these circumstances is to settle for continuing in the same way. If you do this, nothing will change. Of course, you must want to alter the way you behave, and you must believe that you can. The bedrock of this kind of confidence is self-knowledge and understanding. The next chapter takes you through the steps that will lead you to confident assertion in every area of your life.

3

How to Behave Assertively –
Steps to Assertive Behaviour

Acquiring self-knowledge

Identify and acknowledge your feelings

A vital first step on the road to assertive behaviour is learning to recognize and own your emotional state and what you are feeling about people and situations. When you understand and acknowledge your feelings and emotions you are in a position to communicate them. You can also change them if you choose to, in order to get yourself in an assertive frame of mind.

Another important aspect of becoming emotionally aware is that you can become skilled at understanding other people's emotional states and see situations from their point of view.

Listen to your gut reaction

A good way of identifying your feelings is listening to your 'gut reaction'. Sometimes we stifle this reaction because we feel it is shameful, or inappropriate, or that we 'shouldn't' feel like this. There are occasions when we feel it is easier to let situations continue, because changing them requires effort, and so we pretend that we are satisfied with the way things are.

Scene: Karen tunes into her feelings

Karen is speaking with her mother-in-law June on the phone.

'So I'll expect you both as usual on Sunday?' June asks.

Karen stifles the pang of annoyance and resentment she feels and says, 'Yes, of course.'

Karen's instinctive reaction indicates her true feelings, which she does not want to acknowledge because she thinks that she should not resent the fact that they spend every Sunday with her mother-in-law. Karen tells herself that there is no real reason why they should discontinue this pattern, that there is nothing much else they would be doing, and anyway it is their duty to be kind to

June. She even jokes with her friends and says that at least she and her husband get a good lunch once a week.

Karen will be able to make assertive choices in this situation only if she recognizes and owns her real feelings about it. She may still decide to continue with the visits. The point is that if she learns to understand and trust her emotions she will be in a good position to handle this and other situations confidently and positively.

Exercise: Tune into your feelings

For a period of one week, identify and jot down your 'gut reaction' in the following situations:

Someone asks you a favour.
You ask someone for a favour.
Someone does you a favour.
A friend tells you about a recent success such as a job promotion or lottery win.
Someone does not return your call or email.
Someone cancels an appointment at the last minute.
You have an argument with a friend or family member.
Someone pushes in front of you in a queue.
Someone cuts you up on a motorway.
Someone pays you a compliment.
You are not satisfied with work or service you have paid for.
You receive an invitation.

Listen to your body

Sometimes your physical reactions tell you what your real feelings are. When we are angry or scared we experience tense muscles and an increased heartbeat; when we are disappointed or hurt our eyes fill with tears. Your body tells you when you are feeling under pressure. The warning signs will be different for everyone – you might have an upset stomach, while someone else may get headaches. Your stomach might give a little lurch of excitement when you are interested in something, or you may notice that your eyes open wider when you are responding positively to something.

Exercise: Identify your physical reactions to particular emotional states

Feeling	Physical signs that tell me
Nervousness	_____
Jealousy	_____
Pride	_____
Affection	_____
Frustration	_____
Protectiveness of someone else	_____
Feeling out of control	_____
Anger	_____
Fear	_____
Feeling you have too much to do	_____

Identify what you want

It is difficult to explain what you want if you yourself are not clear about the desired outcome. It is surprising how often we do not identify exactly what we want in particular situations, and only realize what it is when the opportunity has passed. Be as precise as you can in identifying what it is you wish to accomplish.

Questions you might ask yourself

Do I want to state my point of view?
Do I want to be listened to?
Do I want to reach an agreement?
Do I want to get something off my chest?
Do I want to have someone's undivided attention?
Do I want to get a commitment?
Do I want to request a change in behaviour?
Do I want to ask for something specific?
Do I want to talk something through?
Do I want to get advice?

Do I want to be reassured?
Do I want to be thanked or praised?

Add your own examples:

1 ———————————————————————————————

2 ———————————————————————————————

3 ———————————————————————————————

Know your vulnerable areas

Everyone has areas of their personalities and lives in which they are particularly vulnerable. These are our 'soft spots', and anyone who pushes these buttons is sure to get a strong emotional reaction. It is important to recognize what these areas are and be prepared to control your emotional response in order to present an assertive reply.

It is natural to be sensitive about the parts of our lives that matter most to us – values, beliefs, people and ideas that are close to our hearts, issues about which we have very strong feelings. These feelings may be connected with our personal history, our families, our jobs and our various social, political and religious allegiances.

Scene: Trisha's soft spot

Trisha is a special needs teacher with a very strong commitment to her students. She is always focused on their welfare and well-being. Whenever she is involved in discussions and negotiations about school policy she is always sensitive to how arrangements will affect her students. Her manager knows that he can get Trisha to agree with any proposal by saying, 'Of course, if this doesn't go ahead, it's the students who will suffer.'

Trisha's instinctive response is to protect her students, and her knee-jerk reaction is to veto any idea that is presented as not being in their interests, and support any idea that is presented as being to their benefit. Trisha could acknowledge this 'soft spot' and decide that in future she will not be ruled by her instinctive emotional reaction and will deal with the proposal assertively.

Your vulnerable areas could be the aspects of your life in which you take most pride and which you feel closely define you – possibly your parenting or other family role, or your professional skill, or your peacekeeping ability, or the fact that you are a good friend. When you are criticized in such an area, your self-esteem and self-image are threatened.

Exercise: Knowing what is important to you

1 What are the important values in your life? Circle all those that matter to you. Add your own ideas if you like. For each idea, tick the appropriate column.
   (a) You pick up references to this idea in conversations, newspapers and magazines, etc.
   (b) You become quite involved in conversations about this idea.
   (c) You get very worked up about this idea.
   (d) You would lose your job or a friendship over an issue connected with this concept.

	(a)	(b)	(c)	(d)
Money				
Achievements				
Material success				
Spirituality				
Religion				
Fairness				
Excitement				
Travel				
Respect				
Trust				
Being a parent				
Power				
Integrity				
Debate and discussion				

	(a)	(b)	(c)	(d)
Love and friendship				
Personal integrity				
Creativity				
Social/political responsibility				
Freedom				
Equality and justice				
Personal responsibility				
Tolerance				
Security				
Love				
Respect				
Loyalty				
Being a son/daughter				
Being a good citizen				

Add your own examples:

1 _____

2 _____

3 _____

2 What do you worry about? Tick the items that concern you most.

Losing status

Growing older

Being physically attractive

Your health

Losing control

Feeling lonely

Feeling rejected

Financial security

Not having a job

Feeling trapped

Not being respected

Not being noticed

Add your own examples:

1 _____

2 _____

3 _____

Do not make yourself a target

Being aware of your vulnerable areas is very helpful in assertive communication. These are the topics that are likely to arouse an instinctive emotional response in you. You can prepare yourself for this response, and remind yourself of the need to stay calm and think before you continue the communication. These are also the areas of 'weakness' that others may spot. You could become an easy target for those who are aggressive or manipulative in their approach, and find yourself at the receiving end of controlling or coercive behaviour. Self-knowledge will help you to predict these situations and protect yourself by preparing an appropriate assertive response.

Your stage in life

There will be certain points in your life when you are likely to be at your most vulnerable and least confident. These points tend to be periods of change and transition, such as major events like bereavement, marriage, divorce, losing your job, redundancy, getting a new job, being promoted. Whether these events are positive or negative, they will still have the same stressful effect.

If you are going through a transition of this kind, remember that you are likely to be in a very vulnerable state, even if you are not consciously aware of it. This could make you something of a target for aggressive or manipulative behaviour. Also, you may respond more passively than you would like because you are expending lots of emotional energy dealing with your personal situation and do not feel up to taking on anything else.

Be clear about your boundaries

Your personal boundaries are the areas of your life that are private and personal to you. These are often sensitive areas, of which others will probably be unaware unless you choose to confide in them. Lack of knowledge about people's boundaries leads to those embarrassing situations in which you tread on other people's toes because you are not aware of how sensitive they are about a certain matter.

External boundaries

External boundaries are connected with your sense of your personal space. This can be physical space, such as the distance you like to maintain between yourself and other people, and your attitude to touching and being touched by others. It can also refer to your feelings about people entering your personal space by, for instance, borrowing your stuff, making use of your work or home space, dropping in to see you, phoning you, sending you text messages or emails.

Internal boundaries

Internal boundaries are the issues about which you are sensitive. They are private to you and are not public knowledge, unless you choose to disclose your feelings on these subjects. A good way to find your internal boundaries is to use your gut reaction. You probably instinctively recoil and feel tense when a touchy subject comes up. You move away, or hope that the conversation moves on before anyone notices that you have gone very quiet. You might feel yourself blushing with embarrassment.

Identify your boundaries

Identifying what your boundaries are is the first step to developing assertive techniques for responding when people cross them. Of course, boundaries are not set in stone and are variable and

42

negotiable. You will let some people closer to you than others, and the situation will change with time and circumstances.

Exercise: Identify your boundaries

Things I don't want people to do:

Behaviour	*Person/people*
e.g. Come round without phoning first	My parents

1 _____

2 _____

3 _____

Conversations I don't want to have:

Topic	*Person/people*
e.g. My own or family's illness	Workmates

1 _____

2 _____

3 _____

Communicating your feelings

Using the right words

Once you have identified what your feelings are, you can learn how to express them. A key skill of assertion is communicating both negative and positive thoughts and emotions. This may take some practice, and you may like to think about the range of words and expressions you could use to communicate the precise nature of your emotional response. If you use words that diminish or understate the intensity of your feeling your message will be less effective, and if you use words the other person doesn't understand you are unlikely to communicate effectively.

Think about the words you normally use to express particular thoughts and feelings. Many of us are in the habit of using expressions that give an overall idea of what we mean and which we know the other person will be able to understand and interpret appropriately. Sometimes, however, this is not enough; we are not precise enough in our communication. We may give the other person scope to misunderstand (perhaps deliberately) what we are saying.

Scene: Debbie is 'cheesed off'

Debbie tells Hari that she is 'a bit cheesed off' with one of her friends who she feels is taking her for granted. She becomes annoyed when Hari doesn't seem interested in talking about her problem, which is causing her a lot of trouble and anxiety, to the extent that she's waking up in the middle of the night thinking about it. Hari does not realize that Debbie is so concerned; after all, she was 'a bit cheesed off' when her bus was late, when her favourite sandwich was sold out at lunchtime, when someone pushed in front of her in the queue at the cinema, and when she failed her driving test.

Debbie could find a more forceful way of expressing the intensity of her feelings, so that her listener can quickly pick up her emotional state and respond accordingly.

Think about the words and expressions you habitually use, and if necessary, find another form of words that expresses more precisely how strongly you feel. You will find this useful if, like Debbie, you have got into the habit of using the same phrase for all situations. This exercise will help you.

Exercise: Matching words and feelings

(a) The words in the list below all express dissatisfaction. For each word, match the feeling described with a situation in which you experienced it. Don't worry if you cannot make clear distinctions between all the words. The exercise will make you aware of how many different ways you can express your feelings.

If you like, use instead, or as well, words and phrases that are part of your everyday vocabulary. Just make sure that you use a range of expressions, and that the people you communicate with understand the meaning of the expressions you use.

angry   annoyed   disturbed   irritated   furious   niggled   upset
resentful   put out

HOW TO BEHAVE ASSERTIVELY

1 A time when I felt ―――――― was when ――――――――――

2 A time when I felt ―――――― was when ――――――――――

3 A time when I felt ―――――― was when ――――――――――

4 A time when I felt ―――――― was when ――――――――――

5 A time when I felt ―――――― was when ――――――――――

6 A time when I felt ―――――― was when ――――――――――

7 A time when I felt ―――――― was when ――――――――――

8 A time when I felt ―――――― was when ――――――――――

9 A time when I felt ―――――― was when ――――――――――

(b) The following words all express pleasure. For each word, match the feeling described with a situation in which you experienced it.

pleased delighted overjoyed gratified thrilled happy elated
satisfied cheerful

1 A time when I felt ―――――― was when ――――――――――

2 A time when I felt ―――――― was when ――――――――――

3 A time when I felt ―――――― was when ――――――――――

4 A time when I felt ―――――― was when ――――――――――

5 A time when I felt ―――――― was when ――――――――――

6 A time when I felt ―――――― was when ――――――――――

7 A time when I felt ―――――― was when ――――――――――

8 A time when I felt ―――――― was when ――――――――――

9 A time when I felt ―――――― was when ――――――――――

The confidence to be assertive

Developing self-esteem

Your self-esteem will develop as you begin to behave more assertively. Confidence in yourself is based on knowing and accepting your personal qualities, strengths and weaknesses.

Exercise: Know your strengths

(a) What do you consider to be your strong points? What are the personal qualities and abilities that you appreciate in yourself? Choose six and write them down. Try to express each one in positive language. Say what you are or what you do. Instead of 'I don't lose my temper' say 'I am even-tempered'. For each one, identify the situation in which you demonstrate or appreciate this good point about yourself.

	Quality	*Situation*
1		
2		
3		
4		
5		
6		

(b) Why not celebrate your strong points? This is a very effective way of increasing your self-confidence, particularly if you have difficulty hearing good things about yourself. Once a day, choose a quality from your list or one that you have added to it, and say it out loud to yourself: 'I was a good friend today' or 'That report I wrote was first-class' or 'I made that untidy, unwelcoming room look warm and inviting'.

Opening up – the art of self-disclosure

Self-disclosure is what we do when we reveal something of our real selves to others. Behaving assertively involves an element of self-disclosure, as two of the basic principles of assertiveness are openness and honesty. Many of us avoid self-disclosure and keep our true feelings and opinions hidden, particularly when we are at work or with people we do not know well. We let our 'real selves' be known only to those close to us. Sometimes self-disclosure is inappropriate and can be a cause of embarrassment, when it is engaged in at the wrong level and in the wrong circumstances. People may be scared off if you misjudge the nature of an encounter or a relationship and reveal too much too soon. Or you may be at the receiving end of inappropriate disclosure – someone you do not know very well pours out the intimate details of a relationship.

Even when you make a well-judged decision to self-disclose, risks are involved. Revealing something of your true self makes you vulnerable and you may fear that others will exploit their knowledge of you in a damaging way.

However, if you have a basic sense of self-esteem and self-worth, you will know that there is no need to fear rejection or a negative outcome. Appropriate self-disclosure is the foundation of meaning-ful relationships, and you will find that communication is strength-ened through the trust that it generates. Also, your willingness to open up encourages the other person to follow suit. The ability to self-disclose will help you to behave assertively in a range of situations in which you need to reveal your thoughts, feelings and opinions.

Types of self-disclosure and levels of risk

Low risk

The least risky type of self-disclosure is when you offer information of a general and public nature, such as:

I've just been on holiday.
I went to the cinema yesterday.

Medium risk

Revealing preferences, likes and dislikes involves a medium level of risk:

I love skiing.
I can't stand too much heat.
I'd prefer an Indian to a Chinese meal.

High risk

We run the highest level of risk when we reveal opinions, thoughts or ideas. Disclosing feelings, emotions and personal values is at the top end of the scale of risk:

47

I really loved that film.
I hate sport.
I support this government.
My family is more important than my job.

Exercise: Practising self-disclosure

If you do not easily self-disclose, choose a suitable context for offering a personal statement at each of the risk levels. Start with the easiest and move up.

Feeling calm

You will not be able to communicate assertively if you are tense or agitated. If you are feeling worked up or anxious, deliberate relaxation can help you achieve a state of calm. There are some breathing and relaxation techniques that you can do unobtrusively in any situation, and they really will help you to control the way you react.

Breathe properly

The old advice to 'take a deep breath' is right – up to a point. Breathing in deeply is the first stage, but the breath must come from way down in your diaphragm, not high in your chest. Use your stomach muscles to control your breathing. The equally important second stage is the breathing out. You should let your breath out slowly and steadily until all the air is expelled from your lungs, then breathe in again. Practise deep breathing regularly so that it becomes second nature to you, and make a conscious effort to breathe properly in situations in which you want to behave assertively. It will help you to maintain relaxed body language and to control your voice.

Exercise: Deep breathing

Take a deep breath and count to five as you breathe in through your nose.
Hold your breath for a count of five.
Breathe out slowly for a count of five.
Let your jaw and your shoulders drop.
Breathe in and out again, feeling your stomach muscles rise and fall.

You can do this exercise before, during and after an encounter. No one will realize that you are doing it, but you will be able to respond with control and steadiness.

Relaxation

You cannot feel or behave in a calm way if your body and muscles are tense. Your shoulders and neck are the areas that are likely to seize up when you feel under pressure. Try to keep these muscles loose by gently rotating your shoulders in each direction. Another helpful exercise is to tighten your neck and shoulders, hold them hunched for a few seconds, then let them go loose and floppy. Stretching is also good for relaxing your muscles. Stretch each leg, shoulder and arm in turn, and feel each relaxing as you return it to its position.

Visualization

Visualization is a powerful tool and one that will help you achieve a state of confidence. One method is to mentally rehearse a situation you are going to encounter, creating a clear, detailed picture of yourself coping wonderfully with it. You can do this at any time, in any place. Just as you switch on a television set, bring up the picture of the situation you will be facing. Mentally see the place, the person or people you will be dealing with. You can keep playing the scene in your head until you have got it just right. When it is right, make the image as big and as bright and as vibrant as you can. Make it glow.

You can lock this picture into your mind and call it up whenever you want to. As you see yourself behaving confidently and assertively, make your own cue to remind you of it. You could link your fingers in a certain way, or form a circle with your forefinger and thumb. Whenever you make this sign, you bring to mind the image of your confident self. The two are linked in your consciousness. At a media awards ceremony recently, one of the winners carried a rose, which he inhaled deeply before making his acceptance speech. In the future, the smell of roses will help him to experience that heady moment of success whenever he wants to.

Self-talk

Positive self-talk is a crucial ingredient for staying positive and confident in challenging situations. We have already looked at ways of replacing unhelpful self-statements with more rational thoughts, and how this enables you to deal with particular situations. Another technique which is good for building your general self-esteem is to make positive affirmations to yourself. The way you talk to yourself inside your own head influences every aspect of your behaviour – so it makes sense to say things that will have a positive influence!

Exercise: Positive affirmations

Add your own ideas to these examples of positive affirmations. Practise saying them each day. Keep adding to the list.

I am a worthwhile human being.
I have talents and skills.
I can be responsible for myself.

1 _____

2 _____

3 _____

Making assertive statements

The power of words – what to say

We communicate assertively through the words we use and also the statements that we make. All assertive communication centres on expressing our views, acknowledging the other person's views, and opening an exchange about what we would like to happen. There are three main components of an assertive statement:

1 **I feel**: My position – what I want, feel, need, how I see the situation.
2 **I understand**: Your position – what you want, feel, need, how you see the situation.

3 **I would like**: I am requesting/would like . . .

Your 'feeling' statement (1) is about your situation, your feelings and thoughts, what you want, where you stand. Communicating how you feel shows you to be open and direct. No one can disagree with the way that you feel. They may not understand it or like it, but your emotional state is your own, and being able to disclose it in an appropriate way is an essential element of assertive communication.

Your 'I understand' statement (2) is about the other person or people: their situation, their feelings and thoughts, what they want, where they stand. The information you give here is based on the information you receive from the other person, through listening to what they say and observing their behaviour.

Your 'I would like' statement (3) is about what you would like to happen. You show how you would like the situation to be resolved, and what outcomes you prefer. This part of the statement leads on to discussion and negotiation, when it is appropriate.

Straightforward assertions

Sometimes you want to make a simple assertive statement about what you feel or think or want. These straightforward statements give the other person information. This information can be a factual statement, or it can express opinions, feelings, wishes, needs, beliefs:

> I'm fed up.
> I'm ready for a cup of tea.
> I love your new hairdo.
> In my opinion, this new system is not working well.

When you are engaged in a longer dialogue, use components (1) and (2) – that is, statements about your position together with a consideration of the other person's situation. These may be expressed in any order. In some situations you will want to begin with your own statement and then acknowledge the other person's position; in others, you may want to listen to and acknowledge the other person's point of view first before communicating your own opinion.

Your 'I' statement

Assertive statements of one's feelings, thoughts, wants, attitudes and opinions are often called 'I' statements. This illustrates the essential point that you yourself openly and clearly own and acknowledge these feelings, which is one of the most important skills of assertive communication. When you say 'I think', 'I feel', 'I don't like', 'I want', you are taking responsibility for your inner state and for communicating it clearly. Using 'I' statements will help you to remain and be seen as calm and non-confrontational. You are claiming ownership of and responsibility for your own emotions, without blaming anyone else. You are saying 'I feel this way' instead of 'You make me feel this way.'

This can be quite a challenging step if, as some people do, you associate 'I' statements with being self-centred, or think that speaking in this way is rude and aggressive. It can be, of course – but so can any statement if it is delivered with verbal and/or non-verbal aggression.

It is surprising how often we communicate without claiming our feelings as our own. Perhaps it feels safer and less intense to express ourselves without saying 'I'. However, this habit of speech makes our communication less direct, and we may become so used to it that when we want to be particularly assertive, we find it difficult to adapt our mode of expression.

Making positive assertive statements of how you feel is a good way of building and confirming relationships. Often we keep positive feelings to ourselves, or communicate them non-verbally, assuming that the other person will understand. Think how much more powerful it would be to express good feelings with 'I' statements:

I'm so pleased with the good job you've done here.
I like the way you are patient with the children.

Scene: Tanya begins to say 'I'
Tanya knows her feelings and responses, but finds it difficult to express them directly. She comes out of the cinema with a friend and says, 'That was a bit slow, wasn't it?' or 'That was a laugh!' When she feels strongly about an issue, she says things like, 'It's just not right to do that!'

Tanya's feelings are clear, but her way of communicating them creates a distance between her and the opinions she is expressing. Tanya wants to be more assertive in certain situations, and she begins by consciously using 'I' statements in unchallenging circumstances, so that she can get used to this way of speaking.

She says, 'I found the film a bit slow. What did you think?' and 'I don't think it is right to behave like that.' She is aware that her communication is much stronger and more positive, and that she gets a more positive response from others.

Statements of feeling

Sometimes we have no problem with saying what we want or what we think, but shy away from the concept of 'feeling'. We associate the word with deep emotion of a kind which we would share only with those closest to us. While it is true that there are circumstances in which a disclosure of our emotional state is not appropriate – expressions of extreme emotion may be out of place at work, for example – nevertheless a declaration of feeling rather than of thought or intention is a powerful assertive tool. Disclosing that you feel, say, disappointed, or apprehensive, or delighted, or embarrassed makes your communication more meaningful. You allow yourself to be more fully known, and this openness and trust encourages others to communicate in a similar way. In any case, sometimes people who are unwilling to express their feelings verbally have no difficulty at all in communicating strong feeling through their body language – slamming doors, frowning or punching the air in triumph.

Exercise: Becoming used to 'I' statements

(a) Practise making statements which start with 'I'. Not only will this help you to become used to speaking in a different way, but in the process you will also become used to identifying your feelings. Add some examples of your own to the ones below.

Instead of:	Try:
You cleaned your room well.	I'm pleased with the way you cleaned your room.
Is it a bit chilly in here?	I'm feeling a bit chilly – how about you?
Any chance of you doing my shift for me?	I'd really appreciate you doing my shift for me.

You've left your sports stuff in the hall again.	I'd like you to pick up your sports stuff.
That was a good evening.	I really enjoyed your company tonight.

Add your own examples:

1 _____

2 _____

3 _____

(b) At appropriate points during the day, take a few moments to identify how you are feeling. A good time might be after a difficult encounter, or when you have really enjoyed something. Find the words to describe exactly what you are feeling, then make an 'I' statement out loud to yourself, for example:

> After that conversation with my manager, I feel frustrated.
> After that session in the gym I feel energized.
> Reading my child's school report, I felt disappointed.
> During this evening I felt left out.

Some feelings that you might identify:

hostility   disapproval   indifference   confusion   anticipation   shame
dejection   relief   helplessness   regret   excitement

Acknowledging the other person

One of the most powerful skills is the ability to empathize with other people. This skill is essential to assertive communication. When you show that you are sensitive to others' rights and their needs and wishes, you minimize the possibility of aggression, and you show that you are considering both your position and the other person's. You see the situation through someone else's eyes, and show that you are willing to listen and to understand. Phrases that show empathy include:

I can see you are . . .
I know that you . . .
I do understand that . . .

Check your interpretations

Sometimes you may wish to give an interpretation of how you think the other person is feeling about a situation, rather than feeding back what you know of the person and what you can see. When you do this it is likely that you are hypothesizing from information that you have taken in. In these cases, do not present your reading as if it is a fact, but use words like 'think' or 'imagine' or 'suppose', and ask if you are right.

I imagine that you must be frustrated by the delay?
I think you are annoyed because I went out alone last night.

If the other person says no and why would you think such a thing, be ready to describe the behaviour that led you to this conclusion.

The power of behaviour – how to say it

Assertive body language

Expressing and communicating feeling is not done through words alone. Your whole person is involved. Your message is conveyed through the signals sent by your words, your tone of voice, your facial expressions, your gestures, the way you sit or stand. Assertive body language matches and reinforces the verbal message you are communicating.

Body language and the meaning of your message

If there is a discrepancy between what you say and the way in which you say it, there are three main consequences:

1 Your non-verbal message will be the one that is received, which may not be what you intended.
2 Because you are sending a mixed message you may not be understood.
3 You may be seen as manipulative.

If you use neutral words but say them aggressively, you will be perceived as being aggressive. If you use confident words with unconfident body language, you will not carry conviction.

Posture

Assertive posture is upright, whether you are standing or sitting. Think tall, no matter what your height is. Keep your shoulders down, making sure that they are relaxed and not hunched, and imagine your whole body is being pulled upwards. Don't lean on one leg, or slouch – this gives a passive impression and communicates lack of confidence. Turn your body towards the other person and keep your arms loose at your sides so that you present an open front. If you are sitting, keep your legs uncrossed and be careful not to twist them around the legs of the chair. Lean forward slightly, to show focus and attention, but don't crowd in on the other person.

Facial expression

Your facial expression should reflect and support what you are saying. If you smile while you are saying something serious, you undermine your message. Let your facial expression show your responses to what the other person says. Raise your eyebrows if you are surprised, smile appropriately to show understanding or amusement, frown or grimace to show displeasure.

Distance

Use space assertively. This means respecting others' personal space, and also not allowing people to use space inappropriately. If someone is sitting or standing at a distance that you feel is too far away for the situation, an assertive response is to move yourself or your chair nearer to them, supporting your action with an explanation like, 'I'm just moving to a more comfortable position.' If another person is sitting or standing uncomfortably near, move away, and if you need to ask someone to move away, make a short assertive statement like, 'I'm feeling a little uncomfortable. Would you move your chair further back?'

Eye contact

Maintain eye contact with the other person. When you are speaking, keep your gaze steady and glance away every now and then. Make sure that you do not glance away as you deliver the crucial part of your assertion. If you are listening, do not break eye contact.

Gestures

Use gestures to support your assertions, although you need to control the gestures so they do not distract from what you are saying. A decisive hand gesture can add authority to your message, but it may turn into aggressive pointing or passive flapping. Try not to move your hands around too much. Don't cover your mouth with your hand while you are speaking, and try not to fiddle, as this will suggest nervousness. Nod when you are listening to show that you are following what is being said. Tilting your head indicates empathetic, attentive listening. Try not to shrug your shoulders. This is a commonplace gesture used in all kinds of contexts, but it just might make you seem either aggressive (as in 'So what? Why should I care?') or passive (as in 'Don't ask me. What can I do?').

Voice

Get the volume right. You might need to check with a friend if you speak too loudly or too softly. Volume of a medium pitch is usually the best choice. Of course you may raise your voice when you are being assertive, to add emphasis, but you do not want it to turn into a shout. Be careful not to let your voice rise and become shrill, as might happen when you are under pressure, neither let it sink to a monotone. Keep a calm and steady pace. You could practise deliberately speaking in a lower tone and at a slower pace than usual, so that you become familiar with the sound of your assertive voice.

Pay particular attention to tone. It can be easy to let a hint of sarcasm creep into your voice, or to sound overbearing when you want to sound forceful. Be careful that your tone of voice does not make you sound whinging, complaining or self-pitying, a particular danger when you are describing the effect of someone's behaviour on you. Sometimes when we feel strongly about something our voice seems to get out of control and run away with us. The best thing is to aim for a matter-of-fact tone; practice will help.

Exercise: Getting the tone right

This exercise will help you control your tone of voice. Being able to use a calm, level tone will help you to manage the way that you sound and enable you to speak in a way that is appropriate.

(a) Say the following statement of fact out loud. You should sound calm and neutral. You are just passing on information.

The flight departs from Manchester.

(b) Now say the following statement in the same tone of voice.

You were late three times last week.

(c) When you are satisfied with the way you sound, using the statement from (a) as your guide, say out loud the following:

I would like you to do the report again.
When you give me your figures so late it means that I have to work overtime to complete my report.
What do you think of my suggestion?
You said that you would clean the bathroom, and I've come home to find it still in a mess.

Some assertive techniques

Fogging

Fogging is the name given to the technique of acknowledging what someone has said without actually engaging with or responding to the comment. It is a very good way of controlling your feelings and allowing you to remain emotionally detached. You show the other person that you have heard what was said, but that you have not been affected by the statement. It is particularly effective in dealing with put-downs or critical comments, and for preventing a conversation from going further.

What you do is just agree that what has been said might be true: 'You could be right' or 'I can understand why you might feel like that.' You agree in principle, but you do not give any further explanation, or apologize. You repeat what has been said without giving anything back.

Practise saying 'fogging' phrases out loud in a calm and level tone, and you will hear how this technique immediately lowers the temperature, and helps you to feel that you are taking control of the situation by not responding heatedly.

This type of response gives you time to think. Even if your instinct is to reject or deny the comment or criticism, there may be an element of truth in it. You will learn something, maybe about the way that you are perceived, maybe about the other person's ideas and values.

Examples

'You don't seem very interested in this project.'
'Yes, maybe I'm not showing much interest.'

'I need to talk to you about your appearance. Your baseball cap, for example. I don't think that conveys a professional image.'
'Okay. Perhaps baseball caps don't give a professional impression.'

Negative assertion

This is a skill to use in conjunction with 'fogging', and is a good way of responding to criticism. When you have agreed in principle with what someone has said, you volunteer some relevant information about yourself.

Examples

'You don't seem very interested in this project.'
'Yes, maybe I'm not showing much interest. It isn't the kind of work I find interesting.'
'I need to talk to you about your appearance. Your baseball cap for example. I don't think that conveys a professional image.'
'Okay. Perhaps baseball caps don't give a professional impression. I think less about appearance and more about what I actually do.'

This technique helps you to stay calm and assert your point of view.

Stuck record

This technique enables you to be persistent and hold your ground in the face of opposition. What you do is just repeat the essential point that you are making until you reach agreement, or agreement to discuss and compromise. Just as a needle getting stuck in a record plays the same phrase over and over again, so you deliver your phrase, the main point of your message, over and over again. Be sure that you say it in an assertive and non-aggressive way, and make an empathic statement as well to show that you are hearing what the other person is saying, although you are not going to be distracted by it.

This is a good technique to use when you have a clear and unambiguous message to give to someone who is being bullying, manipulative or aggressive. It is helpful when you are dealing with someone who is a clever talker, who can cloud the issue with irrelevant information and arguments.

You first need to identify what your core message is, and formulate it in a few words.

Examples of core messages

I would like my money back.
I want you to stop calling me that name.
I don't want to be the note-taker at the meeting.
I need to leave on time tonight.

Once you have this phrase ready, use it when the other person tries to argue or get round you with pleas for sympathy or by playing on your good nature. Keep your voice calm and steady. Don't say it more loudly or forcefully every time, but keep a firm and level tone. You can vary the wording a little, but make sure the message continues to be short and clear.

Scene: Gemma makes her point

Gemma is usually willing to help her colleagues at work, but on this particular day she needs to concentrate on getting some figures ready for the finance meeting. Richard stops by her desk and says, 'Gemma, could you look up the Briarsfield details and check these dates? They've been on the phone already today and they're getting impatient.'

'Richard, I need to finish this work. You could look them up yourself, or see if Noni can help.'

'Oh, but you know your way around that file, and if anything's wrong, you're really good at spotting it straight away.'

'It's nice of you to say that, but I need to get this work done. Sorry.'

Gemma uses this technique again in the evening when she arrives home to find the place in chaos and the kids sprawled in front of the television.

'I'd like you to clean up the living room', she says.

'It's mainly Lee's mess.'

'No it's not – that half-eaten pizza and all the DVDs are yours!'

'I'm not concerned with who made the mess, I just want you to clean up this room', Gemma says.

'It's not fair!'

'I'm not saying it's fair, I'm just asking you to clean up this mess.'

'But we're in the middle of watching this programme!'

'Right. As soon as the programme's over, you clean up the room. Okay?'

Notice that on both occasions Gemma holds her ground and repeats her phrase. On the second occasion, she acknowledges what the children say, but is not drawn into a discussion. She also shows that she is willing to compromise.

These are the key aspects that make your 'stuck record' techniques assertive:

- Repetition of the phrase
- Acknowledgement of the other person
- Willingness to compromise

There will be occasions on which you just need to stick to your guns, and others on which you make your message clear, but move on to negotiate. When you negotiate, do not lose sight of your main objective. You may compromise on details and particulars, but do repeat your 'stuck record' phrase.

Some useful ways of repeating the message

I don't think you heard me.
Let me say it again.
Perhaps I'm not being clear. What I said was (*repeat phrase*) . . .

Probing enquiry

This is where you ask for more details about a critical, negative or positive comment. Use open questions to encourage the other person to be clear and to find out if the comment is justified.

Examples of probing enquiries

What makes you think that I didn't check the letter?
What was it about my behaviour that bothered you?
Could you be more specific?

This is a useful technique for bringing out people's hidden meanings and agendas, if that is what you want to do. It is also a way of encouraging others to be more direct and straightforward in their communication.

Scene: The new haircut

Louise says to Marsha, 'Where did you have your hair cut?'
Marsha says, 'The usual place. Why?'
'Oh, nothing. I just wondered.'
Marsha feels unsettled. She doesn't know if Louise is implying that her hairdo is good or bad. Marsha decides that even though she may hear some criticism of her haircut, she wants to get Louise to be clear. She asks, 'What made you wonder where I had it done?'
Louise says, 'Well, I thought it looked different, that's all.'
'Maybe it is a little different. Did you prefer the old style?'
'Not really.'
'Does that mean that you like the way it is now?'
'I suppose I do.'

In this case, probing elicits a positive response. However, Marsha's questions show that she is ready to hear a critical comment if criticism was intended, and her assertive approach sends the message that she wants to be told things directly, and does not want people to hint and make veiled remarks.

Pointing out a discrepancy

This is where you point out the difference between what has been agreed and what is actually happening.

Examples

We agreed that you would spend no longer th
evening on the phone, but yesterday you were t
of hours.

  At our meeting last month you said that I wouɪu ᴗᴗ ᵍ
responsibility. I'm very keen for that to happen.

Responsive enquiry

This is behaviour that aims to find out the other person's opinions,
position and needs.

Examples

I'd like to hear what you think about this.
How will the new situation affect you?

Use this technique often – it is the one that addresses the crucial
factor of listening to the other person and showing that you are
willing to see the situation from another point of view.

Putting it all together

It is helpful to know the variety of techniques you can use, but do
not worry too much about the terminology. Practise these responses
whenever they are appropriate, and as you get used to using different
responses, they will become automatic and natural.

  The wording may seem stiff at first, but you will become used to
preparing and practising your own assertive scripts in your personal
style of communication. Just make sure that the message is clear.

Exercise: How did I do?

When you have behaved assertively in a particular situation, evaluate how
well you did. Give yourself a mark out of ten for the outcome. The success
will depend on what your criteria are – remember, a successful outcome
does not necessarily mean that you get your own way. You could consider
aspects such as maintaining self-respect, showing respect for the other

...rson, and how difficult a situation it was for you to tackle. Sometimes just speaking to someone about a matter you have been putting off is a success!

Situation	What I said	Body language I used	Outcome (1 to 10)
1			
2			
3			
4			
5			
6			

4

Assertive Behaviour in Challenging Situations

Handling criticism and expressing negative feelings

Criticism is a strong word which covers a range of everyday situations, from the comparatively trivial to the serious and significant. Many of us 'criticize' in the natural course of our relationships and interactions. When we say things like 'I wish you wouldn't do that', 'Why can't you get home on time for once!' or 'Why do you always leave things until the last minute?', we are expressing our disapproval and annoyance in a critical way. Sometimes the criticism is put on a formal footing, as in an appraisal or disciplinary interview at work, but often it is just part of living and working with other people. Many of us dislike being critical and shy away from expressing these feelings, perhaps fearful of the consequences. However, it is much healthier to face the situation and offer the criticism than it is to let things fester and build up until, as often happens, there is an unpleasant scene which benefits no one. If handled assertively and effectively, criticism can bring about greater respect and understanding.

Exercise: How easy do you find it?

What are your feelings about giving criticism or communicating your negative feelings? On a scale of 1 to 9, where 1 is 'not at all' and 9 is 'a lot', mark how difficult you find it to give negative feedback to these people:

Your mother	1 2 3 4 5 6 7 8 9
Your father	1 2 3 4 5 6 7 8 9
Other adult authority figures	1 2 3 4 5 6 7 8 9
Older brother or sister	1 2 3 4 5 6 7 8 9
Younger brother or sister	1 2 3 4 5 6 7 8 9
Your children	1 2 3 4 5 6 7 8 9
Your spouse or partner	1 2 3 4 5 6 7 8 9

Your manager	1 2 3 4 5 6 7 8 9
Fellow team members	1 2 3 4 5 6 7 8 9
Someone you manage	1 2 3 4 5 6 7 8 9
Someone junior to you	1 2 3 4 5 6 7 8 9
Someone senior to you	1 2 3 4 5 6 7 8 9
A close friend of the same sex	1 2 3 4 5 6 7 8 9
A close friend of the opposite sex	1 2 3 4 5 6 7 8 9
A not-so-close friend of the same sex	1 2 3 4 5 6 7 8 9
A not-so-close friend of the opposite sex	1 2 3 4 5 6 7 8 9
Your house-sharer or flatmate	1 2 3 4 5 6 7 8 9
Someone contracted to do work for you, such as a builder or decorator	1 2 3 4 5 6 7 8 9
Medical practitioners	1 2 3 4 5 6 7 8 9

Add your own examples:

_____	1 2 3 4 5 6 7 8 9
_____	1 2 3 4 5 6 7 8 9
_____	1 2 3 4 5 6 7 8 9

Asking for a change in someone's behaviour

There are three main elements in giving criticism:

- Describing the behaviour.
- Stating how this is affecting you.
- Saying what you would like to happen.

These steps will take you through each stage.

1 Describe clearly the behaviour that you dislike or would like the person to change

Make sure you know what the real issue is

Sometimes we do not admit to ourselves what is really bothering us. We duck away from tackling the big things and focus our attention on comparatively trivial matters. One problem with this is that you may solve the minor problem, but still be left with the one that really matters and won't go away. You might get annoyed that your daughter uses up the last of your expensive bath foam, or that your son doesn't put his dirty washing in the linen basket, when what really concerns you is that she or he takes you for granted.

Do not worry if it's a small thing

The little niggles in life build up until they become big niggles. Quite often the things that get under our skin may seem trivial and unimportant, but they can have a cumulative effect and turn into problems that sour relationships. Whether it's squeezing the toothpaste tube the 'wrong' way, making a mess of the newspaper before you have read it, not returning CDs to their cases or mucking up your alphabetical system, never getting you a cup of coffee from the vending machine, or making little put-down comments in a half-joking way – these little things can become big. Before you tackle the problem, make sure that it really is just a habit of behaviour that is getting to you, and that you are not transferring your feelings about the kind of underlying issue discussed above.

Be clear about what you want to achieve

It is likely that you want a definite outcome from your criticism, that you want some change to occur or some solution to the problem. Or it may be that no change is possible and you just want to express your feelings. Whatever the case, first of all be clear in your own mind what the purpose of your criticism is, and then be sure to make it clear to the other person.

Be constructive, not destructive

Criticism should be constructive. It is information or feedback intended to facilitate a better situation. The outcome of effective criticism is that those who receive it are made aware of ways in which they can change their behaviour in order to improve or enhance performance or relationships.

Criticize the behaviour, not the person

A golden rule is to criticize the behaviour and not the person. Don't tell someone that there is something wrong with them. If you criticize the person you apply a description that is like a label – the person is thoughtless, lazy, hopeless, incompetent, self-centred and so on. Although you may think the description is accurate and perfectly justified, this is not an assertive or indeed helpful way to give negative feedback. Using this approach is in effect attacking the whole person, and you may well get an aggressive, resentful or defensive response.

Be specific and descriptive

Identify the precise behaviour that is causing you concern. This is a good way of checking that you have a genuine cause for complaint and are not just having a go at someone who is annoying you or getting under your skin. Unless you are asking for a specific change it is possible that you are just venting your anger or dumping your feelings on them. Also, it is easier to change our behaviour than other aspects of our person. There is no point in criticizing someone for a quality over which they have no control. So make sure that you can give a brief and focused description of what is getting to you in terms of their actual behaviour, that is, things that are said and done, or not said and done, and that you do not focus on the person's character and personality.

Scene: The receptionist with attitude

Jane has been observing the new receptionist at work and is unhappy with certain aspects of her performance. They have a meeting to discuss the situation.

'You have a very poor attitude when you are on the reception desk,' Jane says, 'and this gives a bad impression to the people who work here as well as to visitors.'

The receptionist looks annoyed and says, 'What are you talking about? I haven't got an attitude!'

This is not a good beginning. Jane would have done better to describe the behaviour that she wishes to criticize: 'I noticed last week that on several occasions you ignored the phone while you finished a conversation with a friend, and yesterday you were so absorbed in a magazine that you didn't notice someone waiting for attention.' This kind of description of the behaviour she finds unacceptable is clear, calm and specific, stating precisely what is wrong.

Examples

Non-specific	*Specific*
When you interrupted several times and walked out when someone was speaking	When you were so rude at the meeting yesterday
When you are in the middle of something	You get so involved with what you are doing that you forget we have some family rules

Exercise: Being specific

Practise replacing the critical statements you might use with ones that are descriptive and specific.

Critical statement: You weren't very nice to me at the party last night.
Descriptive statement: At the party last night you ignored me and talked to your golfing friends all evening.

Critical statement: You've let me down again.
Descriptive statement: _____

Critical statement: You just don't pull your weight.
Descriptive statement: _____

Critical statement: The trouble with you is you just don't listen.
Descriptive statement: _____

Do not give blanket criticism

Statements such as 'You always leave things until the last minute' and 'You never let me finish what I am saying' are comments we say out of frustration. They are rarely, if ever, completely accurate, and they are likely to elicit an unhelpful response – such as 'No, I don't.'

Of course, if your listener knows how to respond assertively, you might get a reply such as 'Yes, you're right. I do leave things until the last minute. How is that a problem for you?' or 'I don't think that's true. I do *sometimes* interrupt you.' These replies will

69

encourage you to respond assertively, but it is much better to get it right in the first place by describing a specific behaviour and your feelings about it.

Do not use judgemental language

Try not to use loaded expressions or words that suggest that you have already judged the person and the behaviour. Avoid phrases such as, 'You acted like such an idiot last night' or 'You did your best to make me look a fool' or 'When you came up with another of your ridiculous ideas.'

Don't play psychoanalyst

Keep your statement factual. Don't speculate about what could be causing this behaviour, and don't give the impression that you have superior insight into what makes the person tick.

Get the place right

Think in advance about the best place and time for this kind of conversation. At work, unless you are giving a formal reprimand, it might be a good idea to choose neutral territory. The place should be private. Some conversations of this nature could take place over a cup of coffee; this would work particularly well if you wanted to encourage the other person to open up and engage in a discussion about the situation. You could try 'walking and talking'; this can sometimes seem less threatening or embarrassing for the other person, and also ensures privacy as any onlookers would just see two people having a conversation.

Get the timing right

A good time for this kind of conversation is when you have to continue communicating 'normally' with each other almost immediately. If the conversation takes place at the end of a working day, or just before you and the other person go your separate ways, there is the chance that he or she will think over what was said and feel tense about seeing you the next day or after the weekend. It's best to choose a time that enables you to have the conversation and then move on to other topics, so you can demonstrate that there should be no awkwardness between you. (There are some more suggestions about how to manage this in the section 'End on a positive note' on page 74.) An ideal time would be before you will naturally have just a short break from each other, such as just before lunch or coffee.

2 Describe how the behaviour affects you

Make sure the behaviour is a matter of concern for you

If the behaviour does not have a tangible effect on you, then you might wish to question your motives for offering this kind of feedback. The other person might ask you this very question, and you are likely to feel wrong-footed if at that point you have to fumble for a reply, or realize that you are not on solid ground with your criticism. What are matters of concern for you will vary, but they should be limited to things that have a concrete effect on you personally or on the people and areas that are your concern and responsibility.

You might have strong feelings about someone's behaviour because it is based on values and ways of seeing the world that are different from yours. Of course you may wish to influence other people's values, but it would be better to choose a form of assertive communication other than the three-part model we are looking at here. You will come unstuck if you try to tell someone that your outlook is different from theirs and you would like them to behave in a way more in line with your personal values than with their own.

Link your description of the behaviour with your feelings about it and the effect it has

Your description of the behaviour might begin with a phrase such as 'When you ... '. You could say:

When you don't let me know that you are going to be late (*behaviour*) I feel angry and frustrated (*effect*).

When you arrive late for lunch (*behaviour*) I feel disappointed because we will have less time to talk (*effect*).

Last week you were late back from lunch twice (*behaviour*). This meant that Lianne had to answer your phone as well as doing her own work (*effect*).

When you do not phone to let us know that you have arrived safely (*behaviour*) we worry that something may have happened to you (*effect*).

Exercise: Describing behaviour and its effect

Choose three situations where you want to give negative feedback. For each one, write a statement describing the precise behaviour and the effect that it has.

	Situation	Behaviour	Effect
1			
2			
3			

Acknowledge the other person

Show empathy for the other person's feelings. See the situation from their point of view, and base your empathic statement on your observation and your knowledge of the circumstances.

I know that you have a difficult journey to work.

I know you are very tired when you get home.

I know you are very busy at the moment.

Make sure that your empathy is genuine and that you do not give the impression of paying lip service before you get down to what you really want to say. Your encounter will be positive and meaningful if you can see things from where the other person stands.

Include positive feedback

We all respond to praise and positive acknowledgement. Remember to include an appropriate comment about what the person does well, making sure that it is related to the context. If you are speaking to someone at work, don't say that you know he or she is a terrific parent or a wonderful cook. Comment on their usual good performance, or their contribution to the team. If it is a personal situation, for example with a friend, say how much you value your friendship.

3 Reach agreement about the way forward

Ask for a specific change

If you are asking for a change in behaviour, make sure that it is specific, and the best way to do this is to describe what you would like to happen. Remember to stick to behavioural terms.

Make sure that the behaviour is something that the other person can control

There is no point in asking someone to change what cannot be changed. You are unlikely to make this mistake if you focus on the kind of behaviour that involves a choice. We cannot choose to alter some of our physical characteristics; we cannot choose to alter aspects of our genetic make-up or our life situations. But we can control and change our behaviour and our emotional states.

Describe the change in clear, concrete terms

You should be able to give a concise description of what you would like:

In future, then, you will be at your desk by nine o'clock.

So can we agree that in future you will phone as soon as you know that you will be held up?

It is not very helpful to be vague: 'I'd like you to help more around the house'; 'I want you to be more considerate of my feelings'; 'Be more pleasant when you greet visitors'; 'Have a more professional approach'. Choose one or two specific things that you would like the person to do. Focus on this, rather on what they should not do. Expressing our message positively reinforces our point and paints a picture of the kind of behaviour you would like.

Ask for feedback

Give the other person plenty of opportunity to put their point of view and contribute to the decisions about what will happen next. Ask open questions to encourage a response: 'How do you see it?'; 'How accurate have I been, do you think?'; 'What problems can you see?'

Dealing with comebacks

You might get a response such as 'Everyone else is allowed to get away with it', 'We always used to do it differently' or 'You've never said anything before.' Remember your central statement and repeat it. Acknowledge what the other person has said, but do not be drawn into a discussion about it.

Examples

That may be the case, but we are talking about this situation, and what I would like is . . .

You may be right about that, but what I am saying is . . .

That's a discussion for another time. Right now I need you to . . .

Specify consequences

This is where you say what will happen if the behaviour continues. You may not always want or need to do this, but it is important to be specific when appropriate. Don't say things like 'And there will be trouble if there isn't an improvement.' If you have to come down hard, say 'If you do not come in on time/meet the targets that we discussed/respond more politely to visitors then I will have to write an official report/speak to a senior manager.'

Don't threaten

There may be an ultimatum involved, but it should be discussed and accepted, not presented as an overt or veiled threat. The words you use and the way that you say them will make clear that you are specifying a consequence, not a threat.

End on a positive note

Draw the encounter to an end in the most positive way you can. Don't leave the ultimatum as the final point. At work you could follow it up with something like 'But I'm sure it won't come to that. I believe you/we can sort this out and get things back on track.' There are all kinds of ways you can finish this conversation with a friend or someone close to you. Statements like 'I'm glad we've cleared the air' are helpful.

Moving on

If you have instigated the criticism, see it as your responsibility to handle the way you manage the re-establishing of the relationship. It's a good strategy to have ready a way to move the conversation on, especially if you are still in each other's company immediately after the conversation. You could say something like 'That's fine, then. Tell me ... ', and introduce a neutral topic of conversation. At work, you could have something specific to ask, or have a file or report ready so that you both have something to look at. You might say 'Okay. Now, do have you have any thoughts on ... ' or 'Would you take a look at these figures?' Try to make it clear as quickly as possible that you are not going to refer to your conversation again and that there is no need for either of you to feel embarrassed.

Checklist for asking for a change in someone's behaviour

- Identify exactly what it is that you want to change. Make sure that you can describe it in terms of behaviour and not personality.
- Choose a suitable time and place.
- Describe the situation/behaviour.
- Say why it matters.
- Remember the three-part assertion statement.
- Ask for a specific change.
- Ask for and listen to the other person's response.
- Specify positive consequences.
- If necessary, specify negative consequences.
- If appropriate, encourage discussion.
- If appropriate, be prepared to compromise.
- Summarize what has been agreed.

Some useful phrases

What concerns me is ...
It seems to me ...
There's something on my mind that I'd like us to discuss.
How does that sound to you?'

Receiving criticism – different ways of responding

Aggressive

The aggressive response to criticism is to hit back. You can do this in a number of ways, such as coming up with a criticism of your own, along the lines of 'You can talk. What about the way you ... ' This can lead to a slanging match, which goes nowhere and does not sort out the matter that was the focus of criticism in the first place.

Another form of aggression is remaining silent and refusing to engage with what is being said.

Passive

Responding to criticism passively may involve just meekly accepting what is said, whether it is true or not. If the criticism is valid, passive recipients see it as confirmation of low self-worth and they may start putting themselves down. Even if the criticism is unfair, someone who behaves passively accepts it and may even start behaving in compliance with the unfair comment.

Manipulative

Just listening and not saying anything can be a manipulative response. The silence might be accompanied by a shrug and raised eyebrows that indicate 'So what?' A typical attitude would be 'I won't say anything, but I'll get my own back on him/her for daring to speak to me like that.'

Assertive

Assertive people are confident about handling criticism. Although it is never pleasant to receive negative feedback, they know that they can listen to what is said, ask any questions they need to, and take on board any changes they need to make, without any damage to their self-esteem. The most assertive response to criticism is to see it as an opportunity for change and growth.

Listen to what is said

If the person is not very skilled at giving negative feedback, you might need to ignore generalizations or comments about your personality and concentrate on the behavioural aspect of what is being said. If you want to buy time before you reply, you could repeat what you have heard: 'So you are saying that I ... '

If you think the criticism is valid

Acknowledge and agree. This is an assertive response that will help you to remain calm and prevent the criticism from developing any further. What you do is:

- Show that you understand the point that is being made. Repeating the criticism in the terms in which it was presented or in a close paraphrase is an assertive response.

- Agree with what is said.
- Offer a brief apology and/or explanation if appropriate.

> 'You left your wet coat dripping all over the hall. I wish you'd be more thoughtful.'
> 'You're right, it was thoughtless of me to get the carpet wet. I'll take more care.'

> 'You handled that enquiry very badly.'
> 'Yes, I didn't handle it well.'

Show empathy and understanding. For example, 'So you had to stay late and redo the whole thing. I can see how annoying that must have been for you.'

Give a focused apology, if appropriate. Make sure that you apologize for the right thing, which will usually be the problem your behaviour caused for someone else. Don't apologize for being the person who you are. For example, 'I'm sorry that my delay in replying caused a hold-up. I can see that was annoying for you', not 'Sorry. I'm so useless at keeping to deadlines.'

Add a positive comment. If the behaviour was untypical of you, after you have accepted the criticism you could add a positive comment:

> 'I know there were inaccuracies in my report. I'm usually very careful about checking.'

> 'I'm sorry my remarks caused offence. I'm usually more sensitive.'

Offer to put things right. If appropriate, offer to do something to make up, or ask what the other person would like you to do.

If you think the criticism is not valid

If the criticism is unfair, stay calm and emotionally detached. Remind yourself that you can handle this. Repeat the comment to give yourself time to think. Give a straightforward rebuttal, such as: 'No, I don't agree that I am selfish.'

You could self-disclose: 'I'm surprised/concerned/worried to hear you say that.'

You could show empathy with the person's situation and at the same time assert your position: 'I can see it must have been very inconvenient for you, but I do not agree that I caused the situation.'

If you are not sure quite what the point of the criticism is or if it surprises you

Ask for time to think it over. You might say something like 'I'm surprised to hear you say this. I need some time to think it over. I'll get back to you.'

Ask probing questions. If the criticism is vague or not well expressed, you need to ask questions to make it clear. Effective questions to use are:

How, exactly?

Could you give me an example?

Could you be more specific?

If the criticism is valid, these questions are a way to clarify the point that is being made. They ask the other person to focus on facts, and help to establish a basis for continuing the discussion.

Use the 'fogging' technique. This technique will help you to deal with manipulative criticism. By calmly acknowledging that there may be some truth in the criticism, you leave the way open for your critic to continue with a specific request (which may indicate that the criticism is valid and honest, perhaps just not well expressed) or to back off.

'You just rushed in without thinking!'
'Maybe I am impulsive.'

If you think the criticism is partly valid
If there is some truth in the criticism, acknowledge and agree with just that part of it.

'The trouble is you are so unreliable. I asked you to see that Rosa got that message, and you forgot all about it!'

78

'I didn't get the message to Rosa, no. I'm sorry for the inconvenience that caused. But I don't agree that I am generally unreliable.'

Handling positive feelings

Saying thank you

The assertive way to say 'thank you' is to match what you say to the circumstance, and to deliver your thanks warmly and confidently. Often a brief 'Thanks' or 'Thanks for that' is all that is required, but sometimes you will want to be a little more expansive. It is a good idea to vary the length and degree of your expressions of thanks. Do not respond to everything, from having a door opened for you to having someone give up an evening to fix your computer, with either effusive thanks or just a cursory acknowledgement.

When appropriate, be specific about what you are saying thank you for: 'Thanks for washing up'; 'Thanks for giving up your time and for showing me how that programme works. I'm very grateful'; 'Thanks for listening.'

Many of us say a courteous 'thank you' automatically, many times a day, and the result of this is that it is usually not noticed. What is noticed is when you omit to say thank you, or to give the appropriate degree of thanks.

Giving praise

Telling people something good about themselves is always a great encourager and motivator. Most of us, it is to be hoped, know what a buzz it gives to receive a compliment or to be told that you have done something well. It is well known that children respond more positively to praise than to criticism, and the same is true of adults. Yet many of us feel we receive more critical than complimentary comments. The reason for this may be that we are all reluctant to give praise. Often we respond positively to someone's behaviour, but do not put our thoughts into words because we do not quite know how to. We feel awkward or embarrassed, and the moment passes, and the opportunity is lost. Giving praise assertively is a skill that can be learnt and practised, and one that will enhance your personal and professional relationships and encourage positive outcomes in your dealings with people.

Exercise: Barriers to giving praise

Tick any of the statements that apply to you.

I do not easily give praise because:

I feel awkward.
I feel embarrassed.
I don't know how to express myself.
The other person will feel embarrassed.
They will think that I'm trying to curry favour.
I will sound insincere.
It's patronizing.
There's no point in praising people just for doing their job.

Add your own examples:

1 _____

2 _____

3 _____

Overcoming barriers to giving praise

The feelings that prevent you from giving praise can be overcome. Giving positive feedback at the right time to the right person in the right way has only positive results, and should have a high place in your repertoire of assertiveness skills.

Start with self-talk

Use the techniques we looked at earlier to change your way of thinking about giving praise. The ideas that you have are probably based on faulty or distorted thinking. Choose some of the attitudes that you have identified as holding you back, and turn them into more positive statements. You can use the examples below, or devise your own.

Examples

I need not feel awkward or embarrassed because I can learn how to do this.

I can practise choosing appropriate language and an appropriate tone of voice so that I communicate my sincerity.

I cannot decide how the other person will feel. What I can decide is that I will give this feedback.

Your own examples

1 _____

2 _____

3 _____

The right time

The right time is whenever you feel that praise is deserved. When you feel motivated to express approval, don't stifle the feeling, but take a moment or two to examine your reaction. Check that your desire to give this feedback is sincere and authentic. Then acknowledge and own your response and decide what precisely has impressed you. Focus on the behaviour that you like or admire and think in terms of what the person has done well. Be specific. Vague comments such as 'You did a good job' or 'That went well' are nice to receive but are not nearly as powerful as comments which identify exactly what was good about it.

Vague	*Specific*
Your talk was good.	Your talk was good. I loved the personal anecdotes.
Well done for tidying your bedroom.	Well done for doing such a thorough job on your bedroom.
You handled that person really well.	I was impressed with the patient and tactful way you dealt with that person.
Your homework project looks good.	You put lots of effort into that project – well done.

The right person

Give praise directly to the person concerned. Sometimes when we are impressed by something we tell a third party: 'Didn't Anthea make a good case at the meeting? I had no idea she could be so eloquent!' This enhances the person's reputation, but does not give her direct acknowledgement. As you grow more confident you will feel able to praise a wider range of people. At work, give positive feedback to your peers, to those junior to you and to your bosses. Everyone is human, and everyone likes to know when they have done something good.

The right way

Face to face. You are offering this piece of information as if you were offering a gift. Get the person's attention. When you give someone a birthday present, you do not casually throw the gift in his or her direction as you are passing. So make sure that the person you are praising can pay you attention just for a few minutes to hear what you want to say.

Keep it short. Make your comment brief and to the point, and remember to be precise and specific. The longest part of what you say could be the details of what impressed you.

Positive body language. Maintain eye contact and speak in a warm and level tone. Be careful to control your tone of voice and your facial expression – if your voice and eyebrows rise as you speak, for example, you will give the impression of being surprised that the person has done something well, which may not be the idea that you want to communicate.

Focus on the other person. Refer only to the person you are addressing. Do not turn the attention to yourself by saying how you could not have done it so well. This might be true, but it might prompt the person to give you reassurances about your own performance, which is not the point of this conversation.

Eliminate the negative. Do not say anything to detract from the positive message. Comments such as 'It was so much better than last time' and 'If you had used more seasoning it would have been even better' bring in a negative focus that will lessen the impact of praise. Remember that on this occasion you are offering a short, warm, sincere appreciation of what someone has done well. Measured, critical appraisal of someone's behaviour or performance belongs in another conversation.

Don't drag it out. Do whatever is appropriate to finish the conversation. With a friend or family member, it might be a brief hug; with a work colleague, a warm smile and a nod as you walk away.

Giving compliments

Praise and compliments can be the same thing. You can 'compliment' someone on what they have done well in just the same way as you 'praise'. Often we use the word in a more personal sense, such as when we speak of complimenting someone on their appearance. Apply the same guidelines. It is good to be specific. When you say, for example, 'You look nice today', add something like 'That colour is really good on you.'

Give some thought to the kind of compliment you might give in the workplace. Remember that assertiveness involves judgement and a sense of what is appropriate. Personal compliments at work may transgress someone's internal boundary, and could lead to trouble if they were to be misinterpreted.

Receiving praise and compliments

Apply the same guidelines as above. Just as you would gracefully accept a gift, so you acknowledge and accept the praise warmly and briefly. Maintain eye contact and a warm, receptive facial expression. A smile of pleasure is fine, but not a giggle or embarrassed laugh. If you disclaim what has been said – 'Oh, it wasn't that good!' – or say that it was not your doing – 'It was a team effort really, I couldn't have done it without Jenny' – you are doing the equivalent of returning the gift to the giver saying that you don't want it. Do not rush straight into saying something nice in return, although you might wish to acknowledge the particular value of praise offered by an expert in the same field. For example, you might add to your thanks: 'I really appreciate this feedback from an experienced conference producer/practitioner/manager like you.'

Encouraging people to be specific

You might think that this seems as if you are fishing for more praise, but asking someone to be specific is a sound assertive response. At work, it is helpful to know what aspects of your performance are good. If someone says, 'You dealt with that situation well', you could say 'Thank you for that. What did you think went particularly well?' The other person is then likely to think about it and say, 'The way you sorted it out so quickly', or whatever is appropriate. Specific feedback is helpful on a personal level too. If you are told, 'You look very nice today', you could ask the person's opinion of what aspect of your look is working well for you.

Saying no

This little word is one that causes a lot of difficulty. Many people find it hard to refuse requests and as a consequence end up doing things they don't want to do, smouldering with resentment at the people who asked them and feeling angry with themselves for not having been strong enough to say no in the first place. The inability to say no can have destructive personal consequences, leading to lack of confidence and self-esteem, and also to feelings of being overburdened and under pressure as we end up agreeing to every request and taking on far too much. Our sense of self-worth becomes more damaged as we ignore our own priorities and needs, and our stress levels rise as the demands on our time become unmanageable.

Scene: Maria can't say no
Maria is just leaving her house to go to the gym when her friend Toni phones.

'I'm so glad you're there! Can you come over and babysit for a couple of hours? Gary's been held up and I'm really stuck.'

'Oh – well, actually, I'm just on my way to the gym.'

'Oh good, nothing urgent then. See you in ten minutes?'

'Well, I'd really wanted to go tonight. I'm so out of condition.'

'You can't be – you look great! Thank you so much for this – you're a real friend in need!'

Maria babysits and doesn't get to the gym.

At work the next day Maria's boss asks her to go in his place to a meeting at the company headquarters 30 miles away. Maria knows that the meeting will be irrelevant to her work and she does not want to go. She thinks of an excuse.

'I'm afraid I can't do that', she says. 'My car is off the road.'

'That's no problem. Jill will get you a train ticket and drop you at the station.'

Maria goes to the meeting, kicking herself for having been unable to say no.

Maria's responses may be familiar to you. She makes an attempt to refuse a request, but does not make her point clear or stand her ground. Her behaviour is influenced by her belief that she has no right to say no and that what other people want must come first.

Why we find it difficult to say no
- Fear that we will be seen as incompetent or not sufficiently committed.
- Fear that we will be seen as uncooperative.
- Anxiety that the requester will take a refusal personally.
- Fear that we will be disliked.
- Afraid of hurting the other's feelings.
- Feeling intimidated.
- We like the person who is asking.

Exercise: Difficulties saying no

Think about the people and types of request you find it difficult to refuse. Write four sentences of your own, following these examples:

I find it hard to say no to Genoa when she asks to borrow the car.
I find it hard to say no to my boss when she asks me to take on extra work.

1 _____

2 _____

3 _____

4 _____

When you should not say no
There may be times when you want to refuse to do something, but know that you cannot do so because of contractual obligations or particular circumstances. You have to judge these situations and decide how to proceed. Even if you are technically obliged to do something, it may be possible to negotiate and find an arrangement that suits you better.

Guidelines for saying no

Start with self-talk

Identify the ideas and attitudes that prevent you from saying no. Work out your own statements to counteract these unhelpful beliefs and to assert your right to refuse requests.

Examples

I have the right to set my own priorities.

I am refusing the request, not rejecting the person.

I am not responsible for someone else's feelings.

I have the right to my own preferences.

Your own examples:

1 _____

2 _____

3 _____

Listen to the request

Make sure that you have heard and understood the whole of what is being asked. Perhaps you could respond by repeating the request: 'So you are asking me to work at the weekend', or 'So you want me to pick up you and three friends at twelve thirty.' Repeating the request in a calm and neutral tone will help you to focus on what is being asked and not to be distracted or swayed by the person's manner or tone.

Tune into your reaction

Get used to your physical response to requests and listen to what it tells you. Then think rationally about what is being asked. You may feel a surge of irritation at being asked to pick up your son and his friends for the third night in a row, but the best approach may be to say yes and plan to have a talk with the other parents about sharing the load. Check that if you decide to say yes, it is a rational decision and not one influenced by what you perceive is your inability to say the word no.

Ask for time

If you are taken by surprise or have not grasped the implications of the request, ask for time to think it over. Use expressions such as 'Can I get back to you on that?' or 'I need to think this over.' Depending on the circumstances, you could specify how long you will take to decide and when and how you will let the person know: 'I'll email you by the end of the day', or 'I'll phone you tomorrow.'

Make an empathic statement

Do this when you feel that more than a simple refusal is called for. Show that you understand the other person's position, and acknowledge the thinking behind the request.

Examples

I know that you are under a lot of pressure . . .

It does sound like fun and I appreciate your asking me . . .

I understand that you are fed up and that you would like some company . . .

I know that I have always helped in the past . . .

If the request is in the form of an offer, thank the person for inviting you or for thinking of you.

Give a clear refusal

Follow on from your empathic statement with a word such as 'however'. State your refusal briefly. Don't say that you 'can't' do something unless it really is physically impossible for you to agree to the request. You may be in the habit of using the word automatically. Try to break the habit and use instead words like 'I don't want to' or 'I'd prefer not to'. Make sure that you say the word 'no'. You may find it difficult to say 'no' at the beginning of your reply without sounding abrupt. It is fine to say it mid-sentence, and you might find it easier to put it in the middle of a phrase: 'I know you are under pressure, but no, I won't be staying late tonight.'

Give a reason if you want to, but don't give an excuse

Remember what happened to Maria in the previous scene. She used her lack of a car as an excuse for not going to the meeting, and when that difficulty was overcome for her, she had no choice but to give in

87

unless she could come up with something else to get her off the hook. If you want to test whether you are making an excuse or giving a genuine reason, ask yourself, 'What if this obstacle were removed? Would I then say yes, or would I have to fish around for another excuse?'

Give your reason in positive terms

Try not to use phrases such as 'I have to'. Words like this imply that you have no choice in what you do and that you are not taking personal responsibility for your refusal. You could just drop the words 'have to'. Instead of saying 'I won't be there tonight because I have to visit my mother', say 'I won't be there tonight because I will be visiting my mother.' This is a much more assertive way of speaking and communicates the idea that you take responsibility for yourself and do not present yourself as a helpless victim of circumstances and other people's demands.

Don't give too much detail

If you start to give too lengthy an explanation, it can easily sound as if you are justifying yourself; you can also find that you are talking yourself into saying yes. Have ready a general phrase such as 'I'm fully committed at the moment' or 'I'm afraid I have plans for that evening.'

Phrases to avoid are ones like 'I'm very busy at the moment', which may well lead to a response such as 'Aren't we all?' or 'You're busy! Look at all that Jan's got on, and she's agreed!' Of course you can deal with these comments, but it's better to choose a form of reply which does not so readily invite them.

Say what you can do

Sometimes we do not mean a definitive no, we mean no, not now, or we are saying no to the precise terms of the request. Make it clear if the timing of the request is wrong, or if you would like to negotiate.

Don't apologize

This is a difficult one, because the habit of apologizing is so deeply ingrained that we say sorry when someone bumps into us or spills something on us. In these situations, though, we are not giving a full-blown apology, we are using the word 'sorry' almost as shorthand for something like 'oh dear, never mind', to reassure the other person that we are not going to fly into a rage. Because it is so hard to drop the word 'sorry', it is probably best not to fight the instinct to use it, but to ensure that, in most cases, you say the word quickly, almost like a 'filler', and move on to the rest of your response. The advice not to apologize really means do not include apologetic words and phrases in your refusal. You could say, for example, 'My time is fully committed at the moment, so sorry, I have to say no to your proposal', instead of 'I'm really sorry, but ... '

Use the stuck record technique

Formulate one sentence stating your refusal: 'I won't be picking you up this evening', or 'I'm not coming on Saturday.' Be prepared to use it, in conjunction with an empathic statement, if the person persists.

Useful phrases for saying no

I'll pass on that.
Not this time.
Not this time, but thank you for thinking of me.
I'm going to say no.
I'm not able to do that, but what I can do is ...
I'll give it a miss.
I'm not happy to do that.
I'd rather not.
I'm not prepared to ...

Ways of making it easier to say no

Create a positive background

If you give the impression of being cooperative and helpful, people are likely to accept your saying no gracefully. Think about the way you usually respond when an idea or request is presented to you. Do people see you as someone who looks for reasons not to agree, or as someone who would like to help? If, when someone approaches you with a request, you instinctively brace yourself for what is coming and automatically begin to think of the reasons why you should not agree, your verbal response and body language will give a negative impression. Your response suggests that you are thinking 'What is it now?' You may sigh or make impatient little 'mmm' sounds as the person is speaking, or listen with a slight frown and folded arms.

On the other hand, if you listen to requests carefully with receptive body language, keep your gestures open and your facial expression pleasant and relaxed with appropriate eye contact, you give the message that you want to cooperate. If you always look for what you can offer, whether it is a 'yes' to what the person is asking, or a 'no, but what I can do is . . . ', and if you always show that you respect the person's right to ask, then your refusal of a request is likely to be accepted as a reasonable choice.

Buy time

One of the reasons we say yes to a request then regret it is that we rush in too quickly with our reply. Try these techniques to buy yourself a little time.

- Stall for a few moments as you take in what is being said. A non-verbal ploy would be to drop something, or fiddle with some papers, or adjust your watch strap. You could say something like 'Mmmm' or repeat the request: 'Let me see, you would like me to . . . '
- Spend some time showing that you have understood what has been asked, and the feelings of the other person.
- Think of a way to remind yourself to pause before responding. Choose an unobtrusive personal gesture, something you can easily do when you are communicating with others. It could be touching your collar, or your earlobe. Associate this gesture with the need to pause. Get into the habit of performing this gesture when someone is making a request. It will remind you to slow down and think before you reply.

How not to buy time

Don't try to gain time to think by showing interest in what is being asked. You may be in the habit of asking questions to keep the person talking while you formulate a reply. If you know you want to refuse, it is generally not a good idea to show any interest in the request. Queries like 'Who else is going?' and 'Just how much time would it take?' may be interpreted as signs that you can be persuaded, and might encourage the requester to be insistent.

Never say 'maybe' (unless of course that is what you mean). It will just encourage the other person to try again, or to try harder. 'Maybe' or 'perhaps' or 'we'll see' does not get you off the hook, it just means that you have to go through the whole process again some time in the future.

On the phone

It can be easier to refuse a request made during a telephone call than it is to refuse one made face to face. As usual, listen to your gut reaction. If you feel you would like to say no, it is easy in these circumstances to buy a little bit of time by saying something like, 'Sara, could you hold the line for a moment? I'll be right back.'

Patterns of saying no

If there are certain people to whom you are always saying 'no', and certain requests you always refuse, you might find it helpful to examine the reasons for this. It might be that you dislike the person who is asking. Perhaps the person often makes unreasonable requests, so you have got into the habit of refusing without considering each occasion on its own merit. Consider changing your way of thinking about the person and the request, or initiating a discussion with them. If they keep making requests and you keep saying no, maybe you could make the person aware of the factors that influence your refusal.

Scene: Dionne rethinks her rules

Dionne has a strict rule that her daughter should not go on a sleepover on a school night, but her daughter frequently asks if she can stay over at a friend's house. She begs and pleads, saying that they will get all their homework done and they will go to sleep at a reasonable hour. Dionne always says something like 'No! I've told you before and I'm telling you again, you are not doing that on a school night.' Her daughter then becomes moody and sulky, and Dionne feels angry and frustrated.

This time, when Dionne feels calmer, she tries to see the situation differently. Why does she have this rule? It is because she wants her daughter to have a sense of routine, to take her schoolwork seriously and not to get too tired during the week. Then Dionne thinks: suppose I let her sleep over at her friend's house? Would that necessarily jeopardize these objectives? She decides to give her daughter permission to sleep over if it is a special occasion, on condition that her schoolwork is up to date.

Checklist for saying no

- Use positive self-talk to eliminate any unhelpful beliefs and attitudes.
- Tune into how your body responds to the request. If you get a 'tight' feeling or butterflies in your stomach, it is a sign that you want to refuse.
- Take a few seconds to think about the request and decide what you want to say.
- Gain time by repeating the request, or ask for time to think about it.
- Use an empathic statement.
- Don't over-apologize.
- Give a reason, not an excuse.
- Avoid saying 'can't'.
- Keep your reply short. Don't pad it out and over-explain.
- Say what you can do. Offer an alternative.
- If you genuinely cannot oblige on this occasion but might be able to in the future, say something like 'Please ask me again next week/year.'
- Remember that often you will want to negotiate rather than refuse.
- If the person insists, use the 'stuck record' technique.
- Don't hang around waiting for reassurance.

Exercise: Saying no

Choose three situations in which you would like to refuse a request. You could use some of the situations you identified earlier. In each case, decide what form of words you will use, and what you will say if the person persists. Practise saying the words out loud, in an appropriate tone with appropriate body language.

Situation (a) _____

What the other person will say _____

What I will say _____

Other person puts on pressure, saying _____

I will say _____

Situation (b) _____

What the other person will say ———————————————

What I will say ———————————————

Other person puts on pressure, saying ———————————————

I will say ———————————————

Situation (c) ———————————————

What the other person will say ———————————————

W' at I will say ———————————————

Other person puts on pressure, saying ———————————————

I will say ———————————————

Making requests

Asking for what we want directly and appropriately is an essential assertive skill. Making requests assertively does not mean being pushy or overbearing. Remember that you have the right to request something, and the other person has the right to understand the reason for the request and the right to respond. Depending on the situation, the other person may also have the right to refuse. You will not always get what you want, but making requests assertively will increase your confidence and self-esteem and will improve your personal and professional relationships.

It is likely that you have no problem asking certain people for certain things, but that there are some situations in which you feel uncomfortable. There may be some people you dislike approaching with even a tiny request.

Why we find it difficult to make a request

- Anxiety that the person will feel unable to refuse and will resent us for asking.
- Feeling that the answer will be no.
- Feeling it's pushy to ask.
- Fear of being misunderstood.
- Thinking we will sound stupid.

- Believing that it is impolite to ask for anything.
- Feeling that we will seem weak.
- Feeling exposed.

Exercise: Difficulties making requests

Think about the people and types of request you find it difficult to make. Write four sentences of your own, following these examples:

I find it difficult to ask my manager for a rise.
I find it difficult to ask Darren for help when I have trouble with a computer programme.

1 _____

2 _____

3 _____

4 _____

Guidelines for making requests

Start with self-talk

Identify the ideas and attitudes that prevent you from making requests. Work out your own statements to counteract these unhelpful beliefs and to assert your right to ask for what you want.

Examples

It is honest and open to ask for what I want.
I am not responsible for other people's feelings about my request.

Your own examples:

1 _____

2 _____

3 _____

Decide exactly what you want

Getting it right in your mind will help you to be direct and clear, and to ask in an assertive way so that the other person does not have to read between the lines. Formulate your request to yourself as precisely as you can: 'I want Darren to show me how to work this programme'; 'I want the children to be responsible for keeping their bedrooms tidy'; 'I want us to leave the party before midnight'; 'I want Meera to tell me why I was not invited to her party'; 'I want us to discuss my job description.'

Have a positive attitude

Do not anticipate a refusal. Make sure that you present your request in positive terms. An unassertive beginning would be: 'I don't suppose that you . . .'

The three-part assertive statement

Once you have got your core request clear in your mind, you can develop a three-part assertive statement. It is up to you to judge how much information you want to give about your point of view and feelings and your perception of the other person's situation.

Set the scene. Where appropriate, introduce the topic by flagging up the issue. 'Darren, there is something I want to ask you to do.' This gives the other person time to tune into what you are saying.

Disclose your feelings. This helps the person to understand your request and to empathize with your situation. If you are saying you want to leave a function at a certain time, you might say 'I find it a strain/feel very tense talking to people I don't know', before completing the request: 'so what I'd really like is for us to leave before midnight.'

Show empathy for the other person. People are more likely to listen sympathetically if you show that you understand their situation. You might say, 'I know you have a very busy social life, but I would like us to get together more frequently.'

Don't acknowledge the other person to the extent that you end up flattering and seeming to be putting on pressure – this is manipulative behaviour.

Showing sensitivity to the other person means being aware of the verbal and non-verbal responses that might indicate uncertainty or unwillingness. Of course the other person's reply is not your responsibility, but overriding these signs once you have noticed them could come across as aggressive. Try to reflect what you have noticed: 'You look a bit uncertain. Are you really sure that time is convenient for you?' This opens the way for negotiation and compromise.

Use the stuck record technique

You may need to be persistent. This technique will keep you focused on your request and will prevent you from being side-tracked.

Give a reason

Some requests are straightforward and require few words. In other situations it is natural to give a reason: 'Would you answer my phone for ten minutes? I have to see Don about something.' If you do give a reason, make it short, and do not spend a long time justifying why you are asking. Don't speak passively: 'I wouldn't normally ask, of course, but he's just said that he needs to speak to me urgently, and you know what he's like . . . '

Negotiate

When you are entering into a negotiation, for example at work, you will want to prepare your case, based on sound reasoning and your understanding of the situation. You might say 'Lois, I've been working on this project for six months. I have enjoyed it, but I would like to do something different. Could I move to the Housing Association team? I know they are taking on a lot of extra work.'

Identify what the other person will gain from agreeing to your request, and identify what you want to gain. Present the ideal outcome, but be ready to discuss the kind of compromise you could accept if the ideal is not offered. Show that you are willing to be flexible and to explore solutions.

Accept a refusal

If the other person refuses, accept it assertively. It is a good idea to be prepared for a refusal so that you have a graceful reply ready.

Useful ways of saying 'I want'

I would like . . .
What I would like is . . .
What I am asking is . . .
I would appreciate . . .

What I would really appreciate is . . .
I really need some help with . . .

Exercise: Making a request

Situation (a) ————————————————————————

What I will say ————————————————————————

How the other person might respond ——————————————

What I will say then ————————————————————

Situation (b) ————————————————————————

What I will say ————————————————————————

How the other person might respond ——————————————

What I will say then ————————————————————

Dealing with friends in the workplace

What happens to friendship when one person is promoted over her friends? This is a potentially difficult situation but it can be made easier if it is approached assertively.

Scene: Jill becomes Carole's manager

Carole and Jill are both support staff in a busy office. They are friends in and outside work, and their families socialize together. Jill is promoted to team leader, with managerial responsibility for Carole. Although they have not discussed the situation, each of them is worried about the possible damage to their friendship. Jill decides to broach the subject.

'We need to talk about this new situation', she says to Carole. 'I would be very upset if my job came between us. It will be different at work, I know, but shall we try to keep things the same in our private lives?'

Jill is applying assertive techniques here. She both owns and discloses her feelings, and indicates that she and Carole should accept new boundaries and make some demarcation between work and home.

Carole responds assertively. She tells Jill that she knows she will find it difficult to adjust, but she hopes that if either of them step out of line or get it wrong, they will be able to talk about it and resolve the situation.

In this case, the professional and personal friendship between the women is such that they do not have to lose their close relationship. In other situations, it might be that the new manager has to sacrifice the old times for the sake of the job. You might need to stand back and decide how you should and should not behave in the future. Both you and your team would benefit from your taking a detached view and deciding on boundaries and demarcations.

There is potential for embarrassment when your previous behaviour as a mere team member was less than impeccable. You may have to be assertive in dealing with the collective memory of the way you spent office time surfing the net or taking hours over your lunch break.

Scene: No longer one of the gang

Rick is now the operations manager supervising his former teammates. He has to speak to one of them, Steve, about coming back late to work after the pub at lunchtime.

'Come off it', says Steve. 'You were always late back when you were on the team. And you used to have too much to drink into the bargain.'

Rick knows that what Steve is saying is partly true, and he has to repress his instinctive urge to defend or justify himself. He takes some calming deep breaths and focuses on the point he has to make. 'That may be so, but we're not talking about my former behaviour, we're talking about you coming back late. Be here on time from now on, okay?'

Steve shrugs, and Rick says, 'Look, mate, it's a tricky situation, but in this position there are things I need to do, and we both need to get over any awkwardness about it.'

Rick handles this situation assertively. He uses self-disclosure and the fogging technique effectively, he shows empathy, and he maintains his authority without embarrassment.

Personality clashes

We are all familiar with having to deal with someone who does not like us, or whom we do not like. Sometimes we can just accept and bury the differences between us, particularly if we do not have much to do with each other. However, we cannot always avoid them. We may have to work with them, or they may be members of our family, social or friendship groups. It is difficult to feel comfortable when there is open or covert dislike on one side or the other. If antagonism begins to affect your dealings with the person and you feel uncomfortable about the situation, it is possible that taking an assertive approach will clear the air and enable you to maintain as good a relationship as it can be in the circumstances.

Scene: Maya and Lesley – a personality clash

Maya and Lesley both work at the local fitness centre. Lesley knows that Maya does not like her much. She actually overheard Maya tell someone that she can't stand people like Lesley who make such a fuss about little mistakes. Lesley is in charge of the appointment book, and she was annoyed when Maya misread an entry and double-booked the treatment room. Lesley does not like Maya's slapdash approach and thinks that she is unprofessional. They are very short with each other, and there is an awkward atmosphere.

Lesley decides that she wants to do something about the situation. First of all she changes the way that she sees Maya. She uses calming self-talk: 'That's the way that Maya is. She works differently from me. She has different strengths and weaknesses. If she makes mistakes, I can deal with them professionally without becoming annoyed.'

This makes Lesley confident enough to bring the situation into the open. One morning when Maya just grunts in reply to Lesley's greeting, Lesley says, 'Maya, there's something I'd like to say. I know that you and I will never be the best of friends, but it would be good if we could treat each other civilly. There is no reason why we shouldn't have a reasonable working relationship. What do you think?'

Maya is a bit taken aback, but she shrugs and says, 'Whatever.'

After this things do improve, and they are able to work together without unpleasantness.

Lesley's assertive handling of the situation is based on an acceptance of herself and of the other person. She does not try to make Maya like her, or feel bad because Maya does not like her. Lesley does not blame herself for disliking her co-worker. She thinks about the outcome she wants, and presents Maya with an honest, direct proposal which contains nothing personal or hurtful to either of them.

Apologizing

When someone complains to you about something you have done or said, it is possible that your instinctive response is to be defensive or over-apologetic. Take a few moments to be calm and decide how you should respond. If the most appropriate response is a sincere apology, mentally prepare your reply. Be clear just exactly what it is that you are apologizing for. If you find that you are saying sorry for being the kind of person that you are, you might want to rethink and focus instead on the behaviour that you have shown. Give an apology that matches both the nature and severity of the complaint and the way in which it was delivered. Be clear about what it is you are apologizing for, and why you want to offer this apology.

Apologizing when you put your foot in it

Sometimes, without realizing it, we will do or say something that offends, embarrasses or hurts someone. This can happen when you are discussing a news item or television programme. You make a joke about a certain area of the country without being aware that one of the group has close family connections with that area; or you talk about being on a diet without knowing that your listener is losing or gaining weight because of illness; or you become involved in a discussion about adoption without knowing that the other person has an adopted child. You might realize, by the verbal and non-verbal responses, that you have crossed someone's personal boundary. The assertive thing to do, once you are aware of the situation, is to apologize for being the cause of offence. Do not go through a routine like 'There I go again, always putting my foot in it', or blame yourself for something that is not your fault. You would, however, be responsible for your aggressive behaviour if you continued to press your point once you realized that the subject matter was distressing for someone.

Scene: Tara apologizes

Tara has a friendly and outgoing personality and communicates in a tactile way – she touches people on the hand or arm as she speaks, and likes to give hugs. She is in a conversation with Max about a family problem he has, and she instinctively puts an arm round his shoulders as she expresses her sympathy.

Max draws away and says, 'I know you don't mean to offend me, Tara, and I appreciate your listening to me, but I would rather you didn't touch me like that.' He speaks pleasantly and firmly without smiling and he maintains eye contact. He nods and raises his eyebrows as he finishes speaking, indicating that he does not wish to say any more.

Tara recognizes that she has crossed Max's physical boundary. There is no reason for her to feel offended or angry, or to justify her behaviour with long-winded explanations about that's just the way she is and she's really, really sorry but she didn't mean any harm. Tara simply says, 'Sorry, Max. I didn't mean to make you feel uncomfortable.' She then picks up the conversation where they had left off.

The assertive behaviour shown by both Max and Tara enhances their relationship and helps them to continue positive communication. Notice how Max handles the situation. He does not defend himself or go into long explanations. He says just enough to make himself clear.

Those of us who have ever made a flippant or joking comment, only to hear it emerge from our mouth in an entirely different tone, know how embarrassing this feels. An assertive way of dealing with this is to say something like, 'I'm sorry. That was meant to be funny and it wasn't.' You can use the same response if you have misjudged the atmosphere and made a light-hearted comment which appears in bad taste.

Exercise: Which of the following situations call for an apology?

Your sitting room is in a mess when a friend calls round.
You give someone a lift in your car which is a small model.
You are late for an appointment.

You have started a meeting without waiting for latecomers.
You get a job which your friend applied for.
You forget the name of an acquaintance.

Receiving an apology

Don't feel embarrassed about receiving an apology, or seek to reassure the other person that it's all right. An assertive way of accepting an apology is along the lines of 'Thank you. I appreciate your apology.' This enables you to go on if you need to, or just leave the matter there.

If no apology is necessary, you might wish to point this out, and also show appreciation of the person's gesture. 'There is really no need for you to apologize, but I appreciate your thoughtfulness.'

Making your boundaries clear

In the previous scene, Max made Tara aware that she had crossed a physical boundary. When someone is encroaching on our space, whether it be external, as in Max's case, or internal, we often rely on dropping hints, hoping that the other person will react sensitively to our verbal and non-verbal clues. We may go along with the situation because we do not want to hurt the other person, who of course is not intentionally or knowingly causing hurt or offence. These strategies are unfair on yourself and on the other person. You cause yourself anxiety and frustration, and end up feeling angry and helpless. As you know, a consequence of this could be that these feelings build up until you release them in an explosion of rage that you regret. You put other people in a difficult situation, because they are not to know that you don't want them to behave in a certain way, or talk about certain topics, unless you say so.

The assertive response is to make your position and feelings clear. Do not explain or justify yourself. Use a very few words, and reinforce them with appropriate body language, that is, no smile and a direct gaze.

Scene: Hayley states a boundary

Hayley is with a group of mothers, not close friends, who are discussing their children's recent exam results. Hayley feels very uncomfortable about this topic. She does not wish to discuss her or the others' children in these terms. She says, 'I have to tell you that I'm not happy discussing our kids' exam results. Can we talk about something else?'

Does Hayley feel this way because her child has not done well, or because her child *has* done well? None of your business.

Interviews, meetings and presentations

For many of us, these occasions have several aspects in common – you feel as if you are on display, with people looking at you and listening to you. You feel tense and wound up and you hope that nothing will go wrong. When it doesn't go as planned, for example, you are asked a question you cannot answer, or you drop your notes on the floor, or you can't get your Power Point presentation to work, you feel that you are making a fool of yourself in front of everybody. An assertive approach will help you to deal confidently with any situation.

Use self-talk to prepare yourself

Take each element of your concerns and turn your negative thinking into a positive, realistic statement.

Negative	Positive
They will all be looking at me.	Yes, they will. I will make sure that my appearance is appropriate, and I will practise confident body language.
I'm going to look stupid.	No, I'm not. I will look pleasantly confident. I can learn how to.
They're just waiting to catch me out.	Why would they be? I have been invited to the interview. They want to see me.
Some people on the panel or in the audience won't like me and will feel negative towards me.	That's possible. But most of them will not have strong feelings, and some of them may feel very positive towards me.

Anticipate problems and decide how you will handle them

Use the visualization technique described earlier, and mentally rehearse the situation. Stop at each point where you think that something might go wrong, and decide what you will do and what you will say. Play that part of the scene over and over again until you are confident about your ability to handle the situation.

Exercise: Putting it into practice

How would you deal with the following situations? In each case, think about the outcome you would like, and work out the statement you will make.

Situation: Telling your doctor that you would like a second opinion or that you are not satisfied with his or her diagnosis.
What I could say _____

Situation: Telling your hairdresser that you don't like they way he or she has cut your hair.
What I could say _____

Situation: Querying a comment or grade on your child's school report.
What I could say _____

Situation: You invited your friends to stay with you while their house is being extended. It is taking longer than anticipated, and although you have plenty of room for them, you want them to go.
What I could say _____

Situation: Your child's friend is behaving unkindly towards him or her. You decide to talk to the friend's mother about the situation.
What I could say _____

Situation: You are looking forward to seeing a film or going on holiday on your own. Your friend asks to join you.
What I could say _____

Situation: You strongly disapprove of something a friend has done.
What I could say ―――――――――――――――――――――――

Situation: Your mind goes blank when you are asked a question at an interview.
What I could say ―――――――――――――――――――――――

Situation: Someone makes a joke that you find very offensive.
What I could say ―――――――――――――――――――――――

Situation: Your friend has bought an outfit for an important occasion. It looks awful.
What I could say―――――――――――――――――――――――

Situation: Your partner or significant other forgets your birthday.
What I could say ―――――――――――――――――――――――

Situation: Your boss asks you to tell a little white lie for him. You don't want to do this.
What I could say ―――――――――――――――――――――――

Situation: Your friend wants you to tell a little white lie for her. You don't want to do this.
What I could say ―――――――――――――――――――――――

5

Dealing with Non-assertive Behaviour – How to Handle Difficult People

Dealing with people who are not themselves assertive presents a number of challenges. The golden rule is not to give in to difficult behaviour. If you do, you send the message that such behaviour works, and all that happens is that the person will continue to display it. If you handle difficult people and situations assertively you show that you recognize the way they are behaving and the effect it is having, and that you will challenge it.

A good starting point is to acknowledge what you can and what you can't achieve.

You cannot:
make people change their personality.

You can:
influence people into changing their behaviour.

For a successful outcome, you need to:

- Define just what it is you want to achieve.
- Decide on a strategy.
- Give it time to work.

There may be times when you just want a quick fix. For example, the children are arguing at home and you want them to stop so that you can all have a peaceful evening, or someone at work is being uncooperative about a job that needs to be done immediately. In these cases you act to achieve one single objective in the shortest possible time – peace and quiet at home, the work task achieved. In the longer term, you might wish to apply assertive strategies to deal with the situation – the children's arguments or the difficult work colleague – in order to achieve a wider range of objectives, such as preventing or minimizing future conflict.

How to handle pushiness – dealing with aggressive behaviour

Dealing with an aggressive onslaught

When someone is being angry and aggressive towards you the most important thing is to stay calm and not to respond aggressively yourself. Use some breathing techniques to help you to control your physical reaction, and remind yourself that you can respond rationally. Remind yourself that you are not responsible for the person's angry or aggressive feelings. However, do not be so anxious to seem calm that you go into passive mode, because this will encourage the person to continue to walk all over you. Stand your ground and let the person continue for a bit. It is possible that he or she might run out of steam. If you need to, interrupt. This might be to say something like 'Look, you're obviously very angry. Let's talk about this later.' If you sense that the person has become more receptive, make a calm assertive statement. Empathize with the person – 'I can see this matters a lot to you' – and give your own point of view. Keep your voice calm and level. If you say 'but' you imply that you want to get the empathy over with before stating your opinion. Just leave the words out, and find a more gentle link: 'I understand that this report has made you angry.' Pause. 'The way I see it . . .'

If someone is shouting at you, or if you feel threatened, walk away. This is the assertive action to take. You could say what you are doing: 'Ken, you are shouting at me, so I'm leaving. We'll talk later.'

Control your body language, and make sure that you do not show any signs of aggression yourself. Keep your limbs loose and relaxed, and maintain a steady but not threatening gaze. You might want to fold your arms, a gesture which in this situation could provide you with a feeling of protection and send a message to the other person that you are not going to be pushed around. (This gesture will only seem aggressive if the rest of your body language and your tone of voice communicate aggression.)

What if you are the aggressive one?

How to become less aggressive

- Think about the outcomes of your aggressive approach, both for you and for other people. You may sometimes get what you want, but the cost of this is your self-respect and respect from others.
- Change any unhelpful patterns of thinking that could be contributing to your feelings of aggression. If you get wound up about the way things should or ought to be, or the way that people should or ought to behave, you are building your inner aggression. Find ways of thinking that will have a more calming effect.
- Practise calming techniques to help you control your reactions. Use the breathing and relaxing techniques that we looked at earlier. It's very difficult to feel aggressive if you are physically calm.
- Don't react immediately to situations. Take time to stand back and work out a positive approach.
- Use calmer language. Choose a lower degree of anger. Don't be furious, be annoyed.
- Work out which situations and people trigger your aggression. Once you have identified them, choose a course of action. Some choices are:
  - Avoid the triggers.
  - Change the way you look at the situation.
  - Use rational self-talk: I do not need to get angry. I can handle this. I can stay cool.
- Start to follow the guidelines for assertive behaviour.
- If aggression is a real problem for you, it may be a good idea to do some work on reducing your anger. There are many books and courses on anger management which you might find useful.

How to handle a doormat – dealing with passive behaviour

Dealing with passive people can be very frustrating. Sometimes they don't say what they want, then complain when they don't get it. Their inability to express an opinion makes it hard to know their real thoughts or feelings, and so you are never sure if they are happy or not with a situation. Often it can be difficult to work out what they are saying or asking because their speech is full of apologies and hesitation.

Passivity can become a kind of aggression. If you let people's passive behaviour make you feel helpless and frustrated you are allowing them to push you into a situation that you don't want to find yourself in.

The 'I don't mind' response

A common form of passive behaviour is refusing to state an opinion or preference.

Scene: Wendy won't express a preference

Wendy and Stephanie are going out for the evening. Stephanie asks Wendy, 'Would you like to go to the cinema or for a meal?'

There is a film on that Wendy wants to see, and she has had a late lunch and doesn't feel like eating. 'Oh, I don't really mind', Wendy replies. 'Whatever you fancy will be fine by me.'

Stephanie goes ahead and books a restaurant. Later Stephanie hears that Wendy has complained that she didn't want to go for a meal that evening but felt that she couldn't say anything.

Here is just one example of how frustrating it can be to deal with people behaving passively. In this situation, both those involved lose out. Wendy doesn't enjoy the evening, and Stephanie feels frustrated and embarrassed that Wendy sat through something she didn't want to do, just because she did not express a preference when asked. Stephanie now feels hesitant about making suggestions.

How to deal with people who won't say what they want

An assertive way of dealing with this situation would be for Stephanie to tell Wendy her feelings about it, and ask if they can find a way of preventing a repetition. She could say something like, 'When you don't say what you would like or prefer I feel awkward about making a choice because I don't know if it will suit you or not. Could we agree that we will both state a preference and then if necessary negotiate from there?'

Stephanie could also present options in a way which expresses her own needs: 'I'd like to try that new pizza place. What do you think?'

Rephrasing to get a positive response

Instead of asking:	Try saying:
Is there anything I can do?	What would you like me to do?
How was school today?	What went well today?
Did you enjoy the film?	What was good about the film?
Have I made this clear?	What questions do you have?

The yes-person

People who say 'yes' to something when they really mean 'no, I can't', or 'no, I don't want to', or 'no, not now', cause frustration not just for themselves but for others as well.

Scene: Lisa never says no

Lisa likes to please people and feels that she cannot say no to any request. At work Sanjit asks her to drop off a file to a customer on her way home. 'No problem!' she says, although the task will take her out of her way and she is in a hurry. She stuffs the folder in her bag and rushes off.

The next day Sanjit says, 'Did you manage to deliver that file?' Lisa claps her hand to her mouth and says, 'Oh, I forgot! I'm really sorry. I'll do it tonight if you like.'

Sanjit is annoyed because Lisa could easily have said no and he could have done it himself. This is what she often does, promises or undertakes to speak to someone, make a phone call, send an email, then 'forgets'. Lisa's desire to avoid what she sees as unpleasantness or confrontation means that she responds positively to every request without thinking it through and assessing whether she will be able or wants to comply. Far from making her seem 'nice', this behaviour causes problems for her colleagues. It also causes problems for Lisa. She is getting a reputation for being unreliable. Also, she is genuinely upset when she doesn't deliver what she promised, and on the occasions when she actually does perform the task she didn't want to take on, she feels resentful. Lisa's perception that it is unacceptable behaviour to say no, and that the best way to get along with people is to agree, causes frustration and difficulty for everyone concerned, including herself.

How to deal assertively with people who say yes all the time

The assertive way of dealing with this kind of passive behaviour is first of all to recognize what drives the behaviour. People who can't say no are often demonstrating their fear of confrontation and their desire to please others. It is a good idea to invest some time in finding out if the person is able and wants to fulfil the commitment, or if he or she is just being 'nice'. This can be done on the spot. For example, Sanjit, knowing Lisa's track record, could say 'Hang on a minute, Lisa, and think about whether this really is in your direction home/if you really have enough time to detour', or whatever is appropriate. It is important to communicate in an assertive and non-confrontational way. If someone says 'I'll be there by eleven o'clock', and you think this is unlikely to happen, you might respond by saying 'That would be good, but I know you've got a lot to do before you leave and the traffic is very heavy, so how about two o'clock as a more realistic time?'

The martyr

One of the characteristics of passive behaviour is always putting other people first, a tendency that martyr-types carry to excess. They allow other people to take advantage of them and they take on tasks with a show of resignation and self-denigration that masks their genuine feelings.

Scene: Estelle the martyr

Estelle is always the one who will agree to work late, or do unpleasant jobs at home that other people ignore. 'Oh well, I suppose it's down to me again', she says. 'No rest for the wicked.' She says to herself things like, 'If I don't do it no one will. Someone has to do this, so I suppose I'll have to.'

How to deal assertively with a martyr

Do not buy into their behaviour by praising their self-sacrifice. Remind yourself that the person is making a choice, and that there will be a pay-off for that choice. It might be that this behaviour makes the person feel needed or important. He or she might enjoy feeling unselfish. If you get a martyr-type response from someone, you could either ignore it, or say something like 'Of course, you can choose not to do this. It is up to you.'

What if you are the passive one?

How to stop being 'nice' all the time

If your automatic response is to say yes because you see yourself as a nice, helpful person, there are a number of consequences you may face, none of them positive. Other people may manipulate your desire to please, and you may end up tired, stressed and ineffective from taking on too much and trying to please everybody all of the time.

Change your way of thinking about your relationship with other people. Remind yourself that the considerate way of responding to people is to be honest and to acknowledge and respect their position. Here are some approaches you could try.

Self-talk

Repeat to yourself these affirmations, and make up some of your own:

I do not need to be nice all the time.
I can show positive qualities other than niceness.
It doesn't matter if not everyone likes me.

1 _____

2 _____

3 _____

Change your way of thinking

In Chapter 1 we looked at the techniques of challenging unhelpful thoughts. Use this strategy to help you to combat your 'niceness'.

Old thought: He won't like me if I say I can't help.
New thought: It's much better to admit I can't help than to let someone down.

Old thought: Being nice to people makes me feel good about myself.
New thought: Being straightforward, honest and respectful to others makes me feel good about myself.

Old thought: A nice person puts others' needs first.
New thought: I can put others first if and when I judge that to be the best course of action. I have a duty to take care of myself as well.

Old thought: _____

New thought: _____

Old thought: _____
New thought: _____

How to express a preference

If you find it difficult to state a preference or say what you would like, practise in small ways to get used to saying the words 'I would like' or 'I feel like'. Choose insignificant or non-challenging situations.

Choice being offered	*What you could say*
Tea or coffee?	I'd love a cup of tea.
Shall we visit Joan this weekend?	I'd like that/I'd prefer to do it another time.
Shall we eat before or after the film?	I'd like to eat afterwards/I'd opt for before, when it's less crowded.

Practise saying 'no'

Use the guidelines in Chapter 4.

How to handle a game-player – dealing with manipulative behaviour

The silent treatment

Silence is a powerful weapon and a favourite tactic of those who do not want to be seen as openly aggressive. When they do speak it is in virtual monosyllables, often accompanied by shrugs and lack of eye contact: 'Don't know'; 'Suppose so'; 'I'm just keeping out of trouble'. This is a way of letting you know that they are upset without having to articulate it. It is possible that the person can't actually put the feeling into words, either through being unable to express it or through not having identified it.

Guidelines for dealing assertively with sulkiness

A familiar way of dealing with this is to ignore it. Sometimes, however, you may want or need to know if something significant is causing the behaviour. It might be in your interests to find out why one of your team at work is behaving like this. If your child or partner is uncharacteristically moody or uncommunicative you may want to explore the reasons.

- Let the person know that you have noticed the behaviour.
- Encourage the person to speak.
- Ask open questions.
- Don't rush in to fill gaps – give the person time to reply.
- Wait for as long as it takes.

If the person persists in not responding, comment on the situation. Say something like 'There's no point in continuing if you refuse to speak or to say what is bothering you', or 'Something is clearly bothering you. I'm sorry about that.' Depending on the circumstances, you may wish to add a consequence if the behaviour persists.

Put-downs

Put-downs are the little digs, comments and questions that get under our skin. Some of these are just thoughtless comments, others are genuinely intended to be light-hearted or funny but miss the mark. On other occasions the person's purpose in making this kind of remark is to cause you discomfort or embarrassment. This kind of underhand aggression leaves you ill-at-ease and uncertain how to respond.

How to respond assertively to put-downs

Say that you agree

This is an excellent way of dealing with a put-down. By calmly agreeing you take the wind out of his or her sails. Choose this kind of response when it is not worth investing in a more probing approach, for example, when someone is just trying to wind you up: they say 'Late as usual!' and you say 'Yes, I am late, aren't I?'

You may want to acknowledge what the person says before making an assertive statement: they say 'You're silly to feel that way!' and you respond: 'It may seem silly, but that is the way I feel.'

Ask questions

If you give a response designed to prevent a repetition of a comment, but the person persists, you could ask questions to bring out the intention behind the remark. Asking questions will help you to identify if a genuine point is being made or if the person has a hidden agenda. For example, someone says 'Hard at work as usual!' as you are having a cup of coffee. You say 'You're right, I'm not working at the moment. I'm having a cup of coffee.'

If the person persists in making this remark when he or she sees you having a break and it annoys you, you might want to probe in order to get more information. You could ask: 'Does my having a cup of coffee bother you?' If you wish, you could step it up a notch and say 'Your comment sounds as if you think I don't work hard. What makes you think that?'

You can use the questioning technique whenever you are not sure of the meaning of a comment and when you sense that it is meant critically. For example, if someone says 'You're very quiet, aren't you?' you could reply 'Does my being quiet bother you?' or 'Is it a good or a bad thing to be quiet?' This is an example of an assertiveness technique called negative enquiry.

The most direct form of question is to ask the person, 'What are you trying to say?' If you do this it is likely that he or she will back off, and take the question as a warning not to continue. Alternatively, you will be told what is on the person's mind, which will bring the issue into the open and enable you to deal with it assertively.

Say that you disagree

Use this response when someone makes a general comment. Put-downs like this are often in the form of labels. For example: 'It's stupid to say that!' which could be countered with 'I don't agree that it was a stupid thing to say.'

Sometimes you could partly agree, then make an assertive statement. If someone complains, 'You're so slow to pick things up!' you could respond with: 'It is taking me some time to understand this. I'm often quite quick to pick things up.'

Dealing with comments and jokes that you find offensive

You might feel comfortable with a light touch at first – sometimes just an 'Oh, please!' as you raise your eyebrows is enough to indicate

DEALING WITH NON-ASSERTIVE BEHAVIOUR

your displeasure. If the behaviour continues and you decide to deal with it, choose an appropriate place and time to speak to the person. Use a three-part assertive statement to make your position clear. Here is a model that you could apply and adapt to most situations:

Jim, I have to tell you that I don't like your jokes about ...
I know that you do not mean to be offensive, but I find them unacceptable.
Please stop making them!

Letting manipulators know that you are on to their game

An assertive approach is to let the person know that you recognize the tactics being used, and make it clear that they are not going to work.

Scene: Mandy won't be manipulated

Mandy has said that she does not want to be a marshal on the sponsored run. Ruth, the organizer, is not pleased, and she keeps saying to Mandy, 'There's still time for you to sign up, you know.' Mandy says she will not change her mind, and Ruth has become offhand and snappy with Mandy. Mandy shrugs it off, but the behaviour continues and other people are beginning to notice.

Mandy decides to address the situation. She says to Ruth, 'Look, Ruth, I know you are annoyed because I'm not helping this year, but giving me the offhand and snappy treatment isn't going to make me change my mind.'

What if you are the manipulator?

How to become more direct

It could be that you have just grown used to communicating in an indirect way. Particularly with those close to us, we can fall into a pattern of picking up each other's meanings and intentions.

Scene: Ali and Becca communicate indirectly

Becca says to Ali: 'Are you still going to Sara's leaving do on Friday?' Ali says 'Yes – do you want a lift?' He knows that is what Becca is really asking, because they are friends and each understands what the other means. Ali says to Becca: 'Will you be passing the sandwich bar on your way to the dry cleaners?' and she says 'No, but I can pick you up some lunch from the take-away on the corner.'

116

This is the kind of easy communication that is fine with people we are familiar with. However, you may become so used to communicating like this that you find it difficult to be more direct, and you may assume that everyone can pick up your meaning without your expressing it clearly.

Practise direct communication

Think about the kind of indirect expression you use. Write it down, then think of what you could say instead.

> *Instead of*: The garden's looking awful and we've got visitors next weekend.
> *Say*: Would you mow the lawn before the weekend?

Instead of: _____

I can say: _____

Instead of: _____

I can say: _____

Dealing with negativity – handling a moaner

People who are consistently negative in their response to events, suggestions, questions and ideas can have a draining effect on others, to the extent that you might find that you give up trying to communicate with them. When this happens, by implication you accept their view. Typical attitudes and responses of negative behaviour include: 'There's no point'; 'It won't work'; 'Look what happened when we tried that before'; 'Saying something won't make any difference.' Although such people may seem passive, because they are not intentionally doing anything, in fact they can have a powerful effect if you are drawn into or influenced by their negativity.

How to deal assertively with moaners

- Maintain a realistic level of optimism. You may or may not express this verbally, but it is important that you keep a positive outlook as protection against being brought down.

117

- Don't sympathize or encourage the person to continue.
- Don't offer a reason why things are not that bad – this will only encourage them to persist and tell you that you are wrong, or 'It's all right for you.'
- Take the moaning seriously and respond to the topic as a problem to be tackled. Identify the specific source of the complaint, then move the discussion towards solutions. You may or may not choose to offer a solution.
- You might wish to say something like, 'Look, I can see you're feeling pretty negative about things. Perhaps we can talk again later.' A stronger response would be something like 'There's no point in complaining if you/we can't do anything about the situation/can't find ways of dealing with the situation.'
- If someone consistently whinges, you could choose to walk away. You could explain your action: 'Rachel, I'm finding your constant complaining hard to take. I'm taking a break/going to do something in the other room/taking my work over there for a bit.'

What if you are the moaner?

How to communicate more positively

- Change your way of thinking by using some of the techniques described in Chapter 1. Apply the same techniques to help you express yourself more positively and assertively. Identify some of your typical negative comments and replace them with more upbeat responses. If you cannot find a positive comment, a first step to stop yourself from moaning or complaining would be to find something to say that is neutral, or which reflects what the other person is saying.
- Think about situations as challenges or problems to be solved rather than as opportunities for expressing dissatisfaction.
- Say what you would like rather than what you do not like.
- Allow yourself ten minutes' moaning a day. Remember to choose your audience carefully – a friend might cooperate with you on this one. When you feel a complaint coming on, bite your tongue and save it until the allotted time.
- Focus on one thing every day that is positive. Write it down and say it out loud. If it is appropriate, find an opportunity to share the thought with someone else.

When assertion meets assertion

When you are dealing with a person who is behaving assertively you can be secure in the knowledge that your interaction will be open and above board. You do not need to be on the lookout for manipulative game-playing. You might disagree with each other, but each knows where the other is coming from and each is communicating from a basis of high self-esteem and respect for other people.

Just apply the guidelines for assertive communication. Listen to and acknowledge what the person is saying and feeling and give your own response clearly and appropriately. Be prepared to compromise, and show that you want to find a solution. You will meet each other halfway, and whatever the outcome, you will both leave the encounter with your self-respect intact.

A final word

It is up to you now! You have everything to gain and nothing to lose by practising the skills of assertiveness in every area of your life. The key to success is practice. You can do this by yourself, or there may be a friend who would join you in some role-play. You could take it in turns to work on preparing your assertive scripts and speaking them out loud. It is always helpful to get feedback, and experiencing someone else's situation increases your knowledge and encourages you to express empathy.

Remember that you have a choice. Once you are confident about different styles of behaviour you can choose and manage your responses for the best possible outcome. You will find the ability to behave assertively will be of enormous benefit to you and the others in your life.

Further Reading

Back, Ken and Back, Kate (1999), *Assertiveness at Work*, London: McGraw-Hill.

Bishop, Sue (2000), *Develop Your Assertiveness*, London: Kogan Page.

Chandler, Robin and Grzyb, Jo Ellen (1997), *The Nice Factor Book*, London: Simon and Schuster.

Ferguson, Jan (2003), *Perfect Assertiveness*, London: Random House.

Hartley, Mary (2002), *Managing Anger at Work*, London: Sheldon Press.

McMahon, Gladeana (2001), *Confidence Works: Learn to be Your Own Life Coach*, London: Sheldon Press.

Index